Look, Learn & Create

Knitting

A WORKSHOP
101
IN A BOOK

Creative Publishing
international

Creative Publishing international

First published in the United States of America by Creative Publishing international, Inc., a member of Quayside Publishing Group
400 First Avenue North
Suite 300
Minneapolis, MN 55401
1-800-328-3895
www.creativepub.com or www.Qbookshop.com

Visit www.Craftside.Typepad.com
for a behind-the-scenes peek at our crafty world!

ISBN: 978-1-58923-646-2

Printed in China
10 9 8 7 6 5 4 3 2 1

Library of Congress Cataloging-in-Publication Data
Hammett, Carri, 1956-
 Knitting 101 : master basic skills and techniques easily through step-by-step instruction / Carri Hammett.
    p. cm.
 Summary: ""Beginner's guide to knitting, teaching all the basic techniques through easy projects. Includes DVD-ROM"--Provided by publisher"--Provided by publisher.
 Includes bibliographical references and index.
 ISBN-13: 978-1-58923-646-2 (spiral bound)
 ISBN-10: 1-58923-646-7 (hard cover)
 1. Knitting. 2. Knitting--Technique. I. Title. II. Title: Knitting one hundred one.

 TT820.H25 2012
 746.43'2--dc23

                                    2011028090

Technical Editor: Karen Weiberg
Copy Editor: India Tresselt
Proofreader: Karen Weiberg
Cover & Book Design: Mighty Media, Inc.
Page Layout: Danielle Smith
Videographer: Forrest Fox

CONTENTS

Introduction

Welcome to the world of knitting! Knitting is so much more than just a way to make something. You'll soon discover that the process of knitting is relaxing and even therapeutic. The rhythmic and repetitive motion is very calming and restful. Many knitters look forward to their quiet time with needles and yarn as the best part of their day. Knitters also love to share their craft, and knitting groups, social networking sites, knitting conventions, and, yes, knitting books are abounding.

What You'll Learn

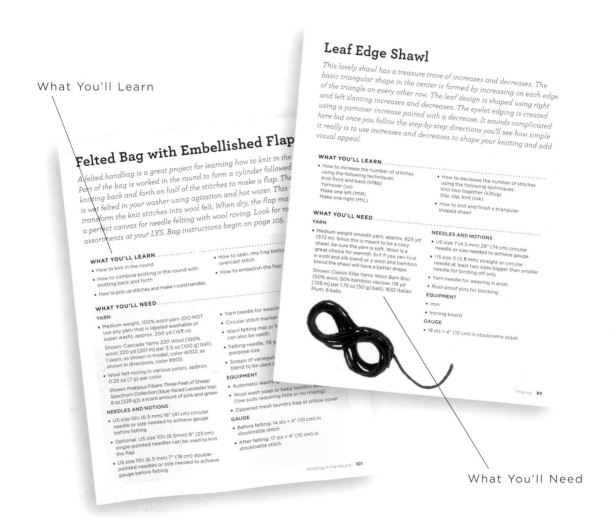

Felted Bag with Embellished Flap

A felted handbag is a great project for learning how to knit in the ⋯
Part of the bag is worked in the round to form a cylinder followed ⋯
knitting back and forth on half of the stitches to make a flap. The ⋯
is wet felted in your washer using agitation and hot water. This ⋯
transform the knit stitches into wool felt. When dry, the flap ma ⋯
a perfect canvas for needle felting with wool roving. Look for ro ⋯
assortments at your LYS. Bag instructions begin on page 105.

WHAT YOU'LL LEARN
- How to knit in the round
- How to combine knitting in the round with knitting back and forth
- How to pick up stitches and make I-cord handles
- How to seam the bag botto⋯ overcast stitch
- How to embellish the flap ⋯

WHAT YOU'LL NEED

YARN
- Medium weight, 100% wool yarn (DO NOT use any yarn that is labeled washable or super wash), approx. 200 yd (183 m)
  Shown: Cascade Yarns 220 Wool (100% wool; 220 yd [201 m] per 3.5 oz [100 g] ball), 1 skein; as shown in model, color 4002; as shown in directions, color 8905
- Wool felt roving in various colors, approx. 0.25 oz (7 g) per color
  Shown: Frabjous Fibers *Three Feet of Sheep* Spectrum Collection (blue-faced Leicester top; 8 oz [229 g]); a scant amount of pink and green
- Yarn needle for weavin⋯
- Circular stitch marker⋯
- Wool felting mat or f⋯ can also be used)
- Felting needle, 38 g⋯ purpose size
- Scraps of variegate⋯ blend to be used a⋯

EQUIPMENT
- Automatic washin⋯
- Wool wash soap or baby laundry de⋯ (low suds requiring little or no rinsing)
- Zippered mesh laundry bag or pillow cover

NEEDLES AND NOTIONS
- US size 10½ (6.5 mm) 16" (41 cm) circular needle or size needed to achieve gauge before felting
- Optional: US size 10½ (6.5mm) 9" (23 cm) single-pointed needles can be used to knit the flap
- US size 10½ (6.5 mm) 7" (18 cm) double-pointed needles or size needed to achieve gauge before felting

GAUGE
- Before felting: 14 sts = 4" (10 cm) in stockinette stitch
- After felting: 17 sts = 4" (10 cm) in stockinette stitch

Knitting in the Round **101**

Leaf Edge Shawl

This lovely shawl has a treasure trove of increases and decreases. The basic triangular shape in the center is formed by increasing on each edge of the triangle on every other row. The leaf design is shaped using right and left slanting increases and decreases. The eyelet edging is created using a yarnover increase paired with a decrease. It sounds complicated here but once you follow the step-by-step directions you'll see how simple it really is to use increases and decreases to shape your knitting and add visual appeal.

WHAT YOU'LL LEARN
- How to increase the number of stitches using the following techniques:
  Knit front and back (kf&b)
  Yarnover (yo)
  Make one left (M1R)
  Make one right (M1L)
- How to decrease the number of stitches using the following techniques:
  Knit two together (k2tog)
  Slip, slip, knit (ssk)
- How to knit and finish a triangular shaped shawl!

WHAT YOU'LL NEED

YARN
- Medium weight smooth yarn, approx. 625 yd (572 m). Since this is meant to be a cozy shawl, be sure the yarn is soft. Wool is a great choice for warmth, but if you can find a wool and silk blend or a wool and bamboo blend the shawl will have a better drape.
  Shown: Classic Elite Yarns *Wool Bam Boo* (50% wool, 50% bamboo viscose; 118 yd [108 m] per 1.75 oz [50 g] ball), 1632 Italian Plum; 6 balls.

NEEDLES AND NOTIONS
- US size 7 (4.5 mm) 29" (74 cm) circular needle or size needed to achieve gauge
- US size 9 (5.5 mm) straight or circular needle at least two sizes bigger than smaller needle for binding off only
- Yarn needle for weaving in ends
- Rust-proof pins for blocking

EQUIPMENT
- Iron
- Ironing board

GAUGE
- 18 sts = 4" (10 cm) in stockinette stitch

Shaping **93**

What You'll Need

It doesn't require a big investment to learn how to knit. You'll need a good instructional book (like this one!), yarn, and needles. Your time investment isn't huge either. It only takes a few hours to learn the basic skills needed to make a simple scarf. Once you become hooked by knitting you'll find that you're eager to add new skills and make items with more complexity.

How to Use This Book

This book teaches you a wide range of knitting skills from the most simple, basic ones to more advanced techniques that will launch you confidently into the full spectrum of knitting options. There are seven chapters, and each one begins by teaching the skills needed to make the projects in that chapter. Each project provides a list of **What You'll Learn** and also **What You'll Need**.

PRACTICE SWATCHES

Especially in the beginning chapters, you will be encouraged to make practice swatches so you can learn a skill before you use it on expensive yarn in the finished project. Buy a skein of high-quality, worsted weight, wool yarn that knits at a gauge of 20 stitches = 4" (10 cm) (or 5 stitches to 1" [2.5 cm]).

(See page 6 for details about yarn). Choose a solid color that is a medium value (not too dark or too light to see details). The yarn used in all the practice swatches shown in this book is Cascade 220 Wool. You will also need a pair of single-point US size 8 (5 mm) knitting needles no longer than 9" (23 cm). (See page 8 for details about needles.)

If you're a new knitter, then the best approach is to start with the first chapter and work your way through the book. You don't have to make every project, but spend time learning the skills and in particular making the practice swatches. The first three chapters—Basic Knitting, Texture, and Shaping—will give you a solid skill set that will prepare you for the remaining chapters, which can be read in any order. Throughout the book, each new chapter builds on the skills that were presented earlier. So, if you read the chapters out of order, be sure to use the index to locate and learn any information you might have missed in a prior chapter.

The DVD included in this book will show you the skills in action and serve as an additional learning tool. If you need elaboration or clarification then consult the DVD. It is both PC and Mac compatible and can be viewed using Quicktime software. To obtain the latest version of Quicktime visit http://apple.com/quicktime/download.

Yarn and Tools

Of all the handcrafts, knitting is the easiest one to bring along with you. That's because the tools and materials are so simple; to get started you really only need yarn and knitting needles.

YARN

Yarn is simply a continuous strand of twisted fiber. The fiber can be anything from naturals like wool or cotton to luxury fibers such as cashmere and silk. You'll also find more unusual fibers such as bamboo, Tencel®, and linen and, of course, less expensive synthetic fibers such as nylon and acrylic. In addition, an abundance of yarns exist that are combinations of all the fibers available such as cotton/bamboo, wool/silk, or linen/acrylic. The selection can be mind boggling, so it may be helpful to find a good, independent yarn shop in your area. The local yarn shop (affectionately nicknamed LYS) is the perfect place to learn about yarn and find reinforcement for the skills that are taught in this book. Yarn shops are typically staffed by expert knitters who are eager to guide your success when you venture beyond what you've learned in this book. Good craft or hobby stores and comprehensive online shops also carry a wide assortment of yarns, needles, and instructional materials.

Texture

Yarn for handknitting comes in a variety of textures and different weights. In terms of texture, you'll find a wide range from smooth to wildly eclectic and bumpy. The photo below shows a range from left to right of smooth (merino wool), bumpy (cotton), boucle (alpaca/nylon), thick and thin (wool), fuzzy (mohair), chenille (rayon), eyelash (nylon), slub (nylon/metallic), and ribbon (nylon). The projects in this book use yarns that are primarily smooth or just a little bumpy because those are the ones that are most manageable for a new knitter.

Weight

Yarn is classified by the thickness or diameter of the strand and this classification is commonly

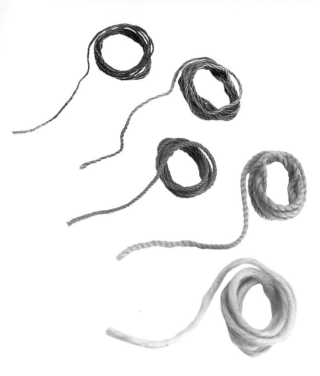

referred to as weight. The thinner the yarn; the lighter the weight. The photo above shows a range of weights from super fine (fingering) to super bulky. On page 34 you will find an in-depth discussion of yarn weight and how to combine yarns for more variety in your knitting.

Yarn Packaging

Yarn packaging (sometimes referred to as put-up) comes in a variety of forms. There are balls (they look like a doughnut) and skeins, which are densely wound and wrapped around the middle with a ball band (label). Both balls and skeins are ready to be used; simply pull the end out of the center.

Another common put-up is a hank which looks like a loosely twisted braid. It's very important to wind the yarn from the hank into a ball before you begin knitting, otherwise it will become tangled. Your LYS will often wind the yarn for you or let you use their equipment. If not, untwist or unfold the hank; you'll find it in a loose circle. Put both hands inside the circle and give a few good snaps outward, then drape it over the back of a chair or ask a friend to hold it. The yarn may be tied in two or three places to keep the hank from tangling. Find the ends and cut or untie the knots. Working with one end, wind the yarn into a ball (like your grandma made or your kitty would play with).

Yarn Label

Learn to read and interpret the information on a yarn label (also known as a ball band). You'll find some basic and predictable information such as the manufacturer, the country of origin, and fiber content. You'll also see the color number and/or name as well as the dye lot, which refers to the batch the yarn was dyed in. It's important to buy enough yarn to make your project, plus a margin for error, from the same dye lot. If you run out and have to purchase yarn from a different dye lot, then the color may not match, leaving a distinct line where the new dye lot starts.

Most yarn labels also include a distinctive square that gives information about the recommended gauge (number of stitches and rows per inch) and recommended needle size (page 9).

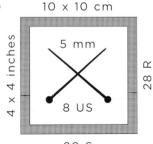

10 x 10 cm

5 mm

4 x 4 inches

28 R

8 US

20 S

Sometimes the square is omitted but you will always find needle and gauge information. The number of stitches per inch is an important number because it defines the weight of the yarn and lets you know whether the yarn is appropriate for the pattern you are using.

(continued)

Finally, you will see care information for the yarn expressed using a collection of symbols specifying how a garment made from the yarn can be washed and whether it can be ironed or dry cleaned.

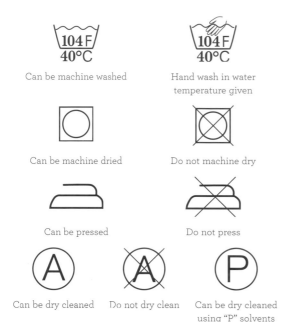

Can be machine washed

Hand wash in water temperature given

Can be machine dried

Do not machine dry

Can be pressed

Do not press

Can be dry cleaned

Do not dry clean

Can be dry cleaned using "P" solvents

TIP Keep a journal of your knitting projects, and attach a yarn label and small yarn sample to each project page. You'll always have this vital information at your fingertips.

TOOLS
Knitting Needles

Knitting needles come in three forms: single point (straight), circular, and double pointed. Needles are sized according to the diameter of the needle shaft, which is the same size regardless of the form (single point, circular, or double pointed). The patterns in the book will specify which type is required. The same advice that applied to purchasing high-quality yarn applies to needles. Don't buy the cheapest needles in the store, and don't use the long, heavy metal needles that were left to you by your great aunt. Follow these guidelines:

Single-point needles: As a new knitter you should use bamboo or wood needles no longer than 9" (23 cm) to 12" (30 cm). Old-fashioned metal needles can be very slippery and heavy and you might find your stitches slipping right off the end. Don't use long needles; they are unwieldly and can cause repetitive motion injuries. If your knitting won't fit on a shorter needle, then you should use a circular needle and knit back and forth (see page 00 or more information on this technique).

Circular needles: At first you may find bamboo circular needles easier to use because they aren't

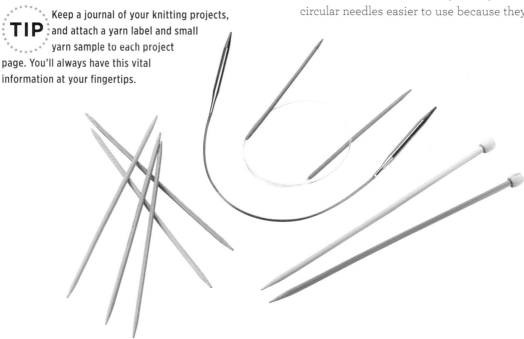

as slippery. But as soon as you feel confident (and can afford them), switch to new, superior quality metal needles with supple cables. You'll find that the cable connecting bamboo needles is often in a stubborn, tight circle. Don't worry about this; the cable will loosen up as you knit.

Double-pointed needles: Look for bamboo or wood double-pointed needles that are 7" (18 cm) long because this is the easiest size for a new knitter to handle.

Needle Sizing

As mentioned before, needles are sized according to the diameter of the shaft measured in millimeters (mm). Since needles are made and sold internationally, the markings can be confusing. Most commonly you will find the millimeter size and the equivalent US size. The most common US sizes range from 0 (2 mm) to 19 (16 mm).

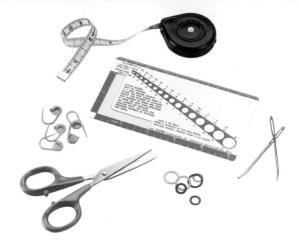

The other measurement is the length of the needle. The needle length is critical for circular needles and is measured from tip to tip (see page 103 for more information about common circular needle lengths).

Essential Extras

There are a few other tools that every knitter should have: a tape measure, a yarn needle (distinguished by its curved point), stitch markers (both closed and locking), a needle/stitch gauge, and scissors.

Handy Extras

As you progress with your knitting skill you'll find that you have more information to keep track of, which is where a row counter, calculator, and notebook come in handy. Stitch holders, cable needles, straight pins, and crochet hooks in multiple sizes are also useful tools.

Knitting Needle Sizes

US Size Range	Millimeter Range
1	2.25 mm
2	2.75 mm
3	3.25 mm
4	3.5 mm
5	3.75 mm
6	4 mm
7	4.5 mm
8	5 mm
9	5.5 mm
10	6 mm
10½	6.5 mm
11	8 mm
13	9 mm
15	10 mm
17	12.75 mm
19	15 mm

Basic Knitting

The process of making a basic knit item is quite simple. In its most fundamental form knitting requires only three steps: casting on, knitting, and binding off. You'll find that learning the three steps is easy and becoming a knitter can be so satisfying! There's a lot of variety that can be achieved using basic knitting by simply changing the needle size, yarn, or yarn combinations.

Garter Stitch Scarf

The first project most knitters make is a simple garter stitch scarf. As you will learn in the Skills section, garter stitch is created when all stitches and all rows are made using <u>only</u> the knit stitch. To make this scarf (page 26) you'll be using a heavier weight yarn than what you use on the practice swatch. The heavier yarn will allow you to complete the scarf more quickly than if you were using worsted weight, and it's a good idea to start exploring different weights and types of yarn as soon as you feel comfortable with the basic knit stitch.

WHAT YOU'LL LEARN . . . .

- How to cast on
- How to knit
- How to bind off
- How to weave in yarn ends
- How to make a simple garter stitch scarf

WHAT YOU'LL NEED . . . .

YARN

- Bulky weight smooth yarn, approx. 230 yd (210 m)

  Shown: Ella Rae *Classic Superwash Chunky* (100% wool; 121 yd [111 m] per 3.5 oz [100 g] ball); color 11, 2 balls

NEEDLES AND NOTIONS

- US size 10 (6 mm) 9" (23 cm) single-point needles or size needed to achieve gauge
- Yarn needle for weaving in ends

GAUGE

- 14 sts = 4" (10 cm) in garter stitch

The yarn should be smooth in texture and a medium value solid color. Ideally, it should also be wool or a wool blend. Wool is far more forgiving for a beginning knitter because its natural elasticity makes it easier to maintain even tension.

The weight of the yarn for this project is known as bulky or chunky. This is a little bit on the thicker side but not so much that it's difficult to handle. When you shop for yarn, look for one that knits at 14 stitches = 4" (10 cm).

Choose a yarn you really like; don't try to save money by purchasing cheap yarn that doesn't excite you. If you don't like the yarn you probably won't finish the scarf, and for your first project success is really important! Also, keep it simple. Avoid yarn with bumps, loops, wild color variations, and fuzz.

Skills and Useful Information

TERMS

Take a moment to familiarize yourself with some common terms and definitions.

Casting on refers to the way stitches are first put on the needle. Think of this first row as the foundation for your knitting.

Long-tail cast-on is the technique used for most of the projects in this book. Its name refers to the long tail of yarn that is measured out before beginning and used to make the stitches.

Binding off (sometimes known as casting off) is how the final row of knitting is taken off the needles. Binding off creates a finished edge that will not unravel.

Knitting is what happens between casting on and binding off. It's the process of forming a continuous interlacement of loops that becomes knit fabric. There are two basic stitches that are used in the process of knitting, the **knit** stitch and the **purl** stitch. The first stitch any knitter learns is the knit stitch. It's a great stitch for making scarves, wash cloths, blankets, even garments. Later when you're ready to expand your skills, learn the purl stitch and techniques such as cabling and shaping.

Row is what is formed after knitting (or working) across all of the stitches on the needle. A row can be composed of all knit stitches, all purl stitches, or a combination of both.

Tail is the end of the yarn that is opposite the ball. It's also the residual length of yarn that is left behind after completing various knitting steps such as casting on, binding off, and adding a new ball of yarn or a different color.

Working yarn is the yarn that is coming out of the ball and what you are using to knit with.

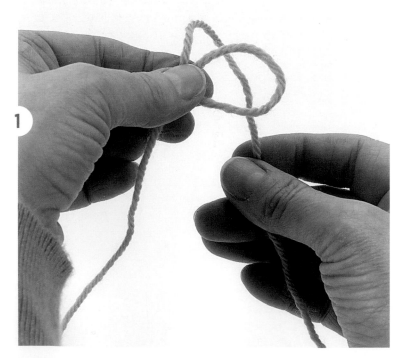

SLIP KNOT

The first step to casting on is making a slip knot. Pull about 30" (76 cm) of yarn out of the ball. The slip knot will be made at a point that is about 24" (61 cm). The tail will be on the left and the working yarn will be on the right.

1 Make a clockwise loop with the working yarn on top and the tail on the bottom. Pinch the loop with the thumb and forefinger of your left hand and use your right hand to drape the working yarn behind the loop.

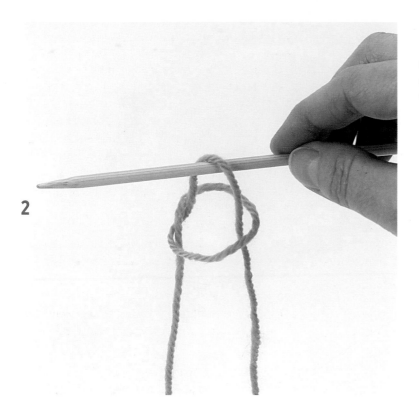

2 Holding the needle in your right hand, go under the strand of working yarn that is draped across the back of the loop.

3 Drop the loop from your left hand. Pull the tail and the working yarn to adjust the tension and snug the loop on the needle The slip knot forms the first stitch on the needle when casting on.

CAST ON (CO)

The most prevalent technique for casting on is known as the long-tail cast-on. It gets its name from the fact that half of the cast-on stitch is made using a tail of yarn, so before starting you must make sure your tail is long enough to cast on the desired number of stitches. A good rule of thumb is to allow about 1" (2.5 cm) for each stitch that is to be cast on. You can also wrap the yarn around the needle you'll be using once for each stitch and then add about 8" (20 cm) for good measure.

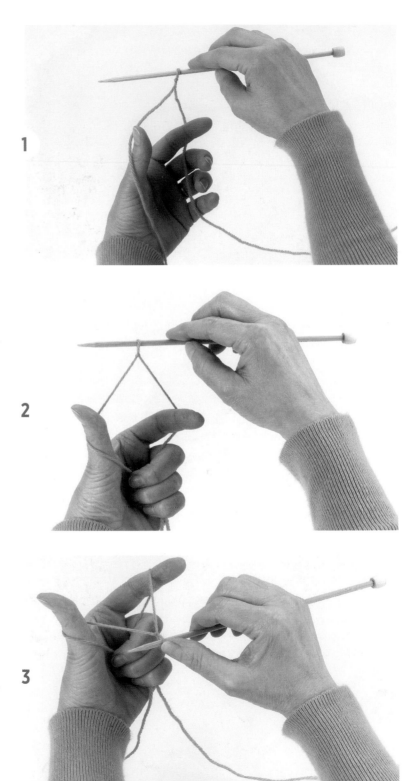

1 Start with the slip knot on the right needle. The tail should be about 24" (61 cm) long, which will allow for casting on about 20 stitches. The tail should be on the left and the working yarn on the right. Coming from behind, put the thumb and forefinger of your left hand between the tail and the working yarn. The tail should be draped over your thumb and the working yarn over your forefinger.

2 Use the other fingers of your left hand to hold both strands snugly against your palm. With the palm of your left hand facing you, spread your thumb and forefinger apart. The yarn will form a diamond.

3 Pull the top of the diamond down with your right hand. Now it looks like a sling shot.

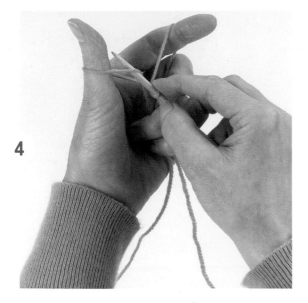

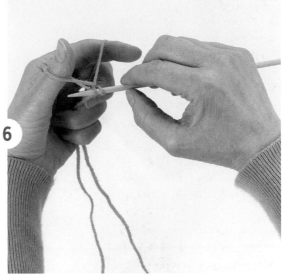

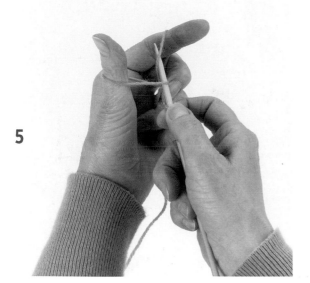

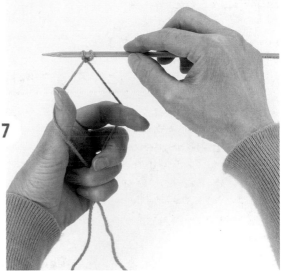

4 Insert the needle upward through the loop on the thumb.

5 Pivot the needle to the right and go over the top of and then under the working yarn on your forefinger, picking up a loop.

6 Pull the new loop down and through the thumb loop sending the needle back the same way it went in.

7 Drop your thumb out of its original tail loop, and then re-hook it on the tail to form the diamond again. A new stitch is now on the needle but it's too loose. Spread the thumb and forefinger of your left hand apart to gently pull the two strands at the base of the new stitch until it is snug (not tight!) on the needle. The second cast-on stitch is now complete. Reposition the yarn in the sling shot position and repeat steps 4 through 7 until you have memorized the motions.

Practice Swatch: Knit (K, k)

Once you have mastered casting on, make a practice swatch using worsted weight yarn and US size 8 (5 mm) 9″ (23 cm) single-pointed needles. **Cast on** 20 stitches and follow these steps to learn the knit stitch.

1. Hold the needle with the cast-on stitches in your left hand with the needle tip pointing to the right. As you work across the row the stitches will be transferred from the left needle to the right needle. The row is complete when all the stitches have been transferred off the left needle and onto the right needle.

2. Hold the empty needle in your right hand with the tip pointing to the left. For both needles, your thumb and middle finger will be lightly grasping the needles. Working from the front to the back, insert the right needle into the first stitch on the left needle (the one closest to the tip) going through the loop just above the bump. The working yarn will be in back of both needles.

3. Use the fingers of your left hand to hold the needles so they form an X (the right needle will be in back).

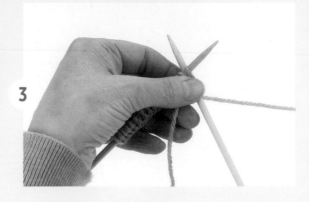

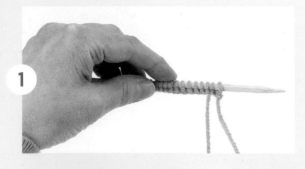

4. Pick up the working yarn with your right hand and wrap it around the right-hand needle in a counterclockwise direction. The yarn will end up between the two needles. Later you will learn some special techniques for grasping the working yarn. For now, simply hold the working yarn between the thumb and forefinger of your right hand when called for.

5. Holding the working yarn (with a bit of tension) and the right needle together, dip the needle down to the left and then toward you, drawing the working yarn through the first stitch on the left needle. The right needle will now be in front of the left needle with a new loop of yarn on it.

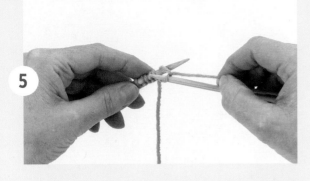

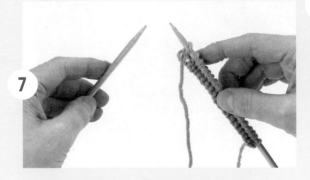

8. Transfer the right needle to your left hand with the tip pointing to the right to begin a new row. Before beginning the new row, gently tug at the bumps at the bottom of the new stitches and make sure the working yarn is coming out of the bottom of the bump on the stitch closest to the left needle tip. Repeat steps 2 through 6 across the row.

Continue working new rows on your practice swatch until you are comfortable with making knit stitches. The style of knitting you've just learned, with the right hand wrapping the yarn around the needle, is known as the English method. You will find information about the Continental method of knitting, which uses the left hand to wrap the yarn around the needle, on page 56.

6. Slide the right needle to the right and off the end of the left needle, taking the newly formed stitch off the left needle. The original stitch will come with it. One knit stitch has been completed.

7. Repeat steps 2 through 6 across the remainder of the stitches on the left needle. One knit row has been completed. Notice that the right needle is now the "full" needle.

BIND OFF (BO)

If you were to remove your knitting from the needles before binding it off, the stitches would unravel. Binding off (also known as casting off) is how the final row of knitting is taken off the needle. Binding off creates a finished edge that is most often quite simple but can also be decorative. In this section you'll be learning the basic, simple version of binding off.

1 Knit two stitches onto the right needle in the usual way.

2 Use the left needle to lift up the stitch that is furthest away from the right needle tip (the first stitch that was knit).

3 Pass the lifted stitch over the stitch that is closest to the right needle tip (the second stitch that was knit) and off the tip of the needle.

It's a lot like playing leapfrog with the stitches. When you are first learning to bind off you may find it easier to lift the stitch with the fingers of your left hand.

4 Knit another stitch onto the right needle and once again pass the second stitch on the right needle over the first stitch and off the end of the needle. Continue in this manner across the row until just 1 stitch is left on the right needle and the left needle is empty.

5 Cut the yarn leaving a tail at least 8" (20 cm) long. Remove the needle from the last stitch and pull on the loop to enlarge the stitch a bit. Reach through the loop with your thumb and forefinger, grab the tail, and pull it back through the loop. Continue pulling until the loop shrinks and is snug against the knitting.

JOINING NEW YARN

As you knit a longer scarf requiring more than one ball of yarn, you will need to join a new ball of yarn. The most important thing to remember is that you must leave a tail at least 8" (20 cm) long that can be woven in when you finish knitting. The best place to join yarn is on a selvedge (side edge), so plan ahead. Simply stop knitting with the old ball of yarn at the end of one row and start knitting with the new ball at the beginning of the next row.

If your yarn isn't too thick you can actually tie the new yarn to the tail of the old yarn at the beginning of a new row. Use the new yarn to tie an overhand knot around the tail and then slide the knot until it rests firmly against the edge of your knitting. Don't pull the bump through the stitch—leave it resting along the edge. You most certainly should use this technique with very slippery yarn.

When knitting with bulky yarn, simply stop knitting with the old ball of yarn at the end of one row and start the new ball on the next row. Some knitters worry about this method since it looks like it might unravel your knitting. You can tie half a square knot to hold the two tails in place until you finish, but untie the knot before weaving in the ends so you don't add a bump.

WEAVING IN ENDS

When your project is completed there will be tails remaining from the cast-on and bind-off (sometimes more if you added a new ball of yarn or worked with several colors). The tails must be secured in order for the knit piece to maintain its integrity. DON'T CUT THE TAILS BEFORE WEAVING THEM INTO YOUR KNITTING!

The tails can be woven into the cast-on edge, the bound-off edge, or the side (selvedge edge) of the knitting for items such as a scarf or blanket. If you're making a garment, it's best to avoid too much bulk in a selvedge edge which might become part of a seam, so the tails are invisibly woven into the body of the knitting on the wrong side, either horizontally or diagonally.

No matter where you weave in the tail, a few preparatory steps are necessary:

- Pull the tail to tighten up any loops or stitches that it's coming from.
- Thread the tail onto a blunt ended yarn needle.

Weaving Tails along the Cast-On or Bound-Off Edge

1 Pass (or weave) the needle through the knit loops along the top or bottom edge for about 2" (5 cm).

2 Then turn and weave the tail back in the opposite direction for about 1" (2.5 cm). If possible, use different loops for the second, shorter section.

Weaving Tails along the Side (Selvedge Edge)

3 Pass (or weave) the needle through the loops along the side edge for about 2" (5 cm). Then turn and weave the tail back in the opposite direction for about 1" (2.5 cm). If possible, use different loops for the second, shorter section.

Weaving Ends Horizontally in the Body of the Knitting

4 On the wrong side of the knitting, weave the needle through the bumps or loops, working one loop at a time. Weave in one direction for about 2" (5 cm)

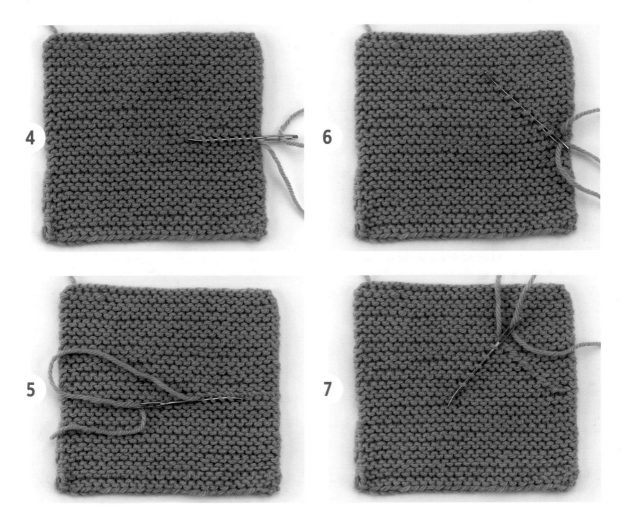

5 Then turn and weave the tail back in the opposite direction for about 1" (2.5 cm). On the shorter section, weave the yarn through the loops on the opposite side of the row.

Weaving Ends Diagonally in the Body of the Knitting

6 On the wrong side of the knitting, weave the needle diagonally through the bumps or loops, working one loop at a time. Always weave through the bottom loop of the paired loops from each row. Weave in one direction for about 2" (5 cm).

7 Turn the knitting and weave in the opposite diagonal direction for about 1" (2.5 cm).

Finally, keep these guidelines in mind when you are weaving in ends:

- It's best to change yarn on the side (selvedge) edge. Avoid changing yarn in the middle of a row.
- Don't split the plies of the yarn when weaving the ends. Rather, go through the loops in the knitting.
- Whenever possible weave the ends into an area made from the same color.
- While weaving ends in the body of the knitting, frequently check the right side to make certain the weaving cannot be seen.
- When you have finished weaving, gently pull the knitting in the direction of the woven-in tails to make sure the knit fabric isn't restricted, and then trim the tails to ¼" (6 mm).

GARTER STITCH

Garter stitch is the simplest knitting stitch. It is created when all stitches and all rows are made using the knit stitch. Garter stitch looks the same on both sides and it is characterized by garter ridges, which can be seen clearly if the swatch is stretched a bit lengthwise (between the cast-on and bound-off edges). The garter ridge is a bumpy, horizontal line extending between the two side edges of the knitting. The bumps are the interlacement of 2 rows of knitting. When counting knitting rows in garter stitch, each ridge represents 2 rows.

Garter stitch is an excellent stitch for a scarf. The fabric is dense, perfectly flat, and its edges don't curl. The simple structure of the stitch allows the yarn to be the focus. It stretches more in length than crosswise, and a scarf made using garter stitch should not be stored hanging but rather folded and left on a shelf.

HOW TO MAKE A GAUGE SWATCH

First of all, what is a gauge swatch? A gauge swatch is simply a small sample of knitting that is made to determine the width and height of your stitches, otherwise known as the gauge. You may wonder why it's important to make a gauge swatch. If you want the item you are making to turn out the way you expect and match the measurements specified in the pattern, then your stitches must be the same size as specified in the pattern. The pattern will tell you what gauge you need to achieve and it will be stated as the number of stitches (and sometimes rows) in an area of knitting that is 4" (10 cm) square. For instance, in the pattern for the Garter Stitch Scarf the gauge is 14 stitches = 4" (10 cm). Gauge can also be referred to as stitches to 1" (2.5 cm), which is simply 14 stitches divided by 4, or 3½ stitches per 1" (2.5 cm).

To make a gauge swatch, use the needles recommended in the pattern and cast on the number of stitches in the gauge swatch plus two to four. Since the edge stitches are usually uneven, the gauge should be measured at least 1 or 2 stitches in from the edge. Knit at least 4" (10 cm)

in the stitch pattern specified for the gauge in the project instructions. It's important that you make your swatch using the stitch specified. Don't be tempted to measure the swatch after just a few rows of knitting. It's important to "settle in" to your knitting with the new yarn and needles.

What if your swatch doesn't match the size specified in the knitting? If the swatch is wider than 4" (10 cm) then your stitches are too big. If the swatch is narrower than 4" (10 cm) then your stitches are too small. If your stitches are too big, then you need to use smaller needles; if your stitches are too small, then you need to use larger needles.

The most important thing to learn about gauge is that you don't have to use the needle that is called for in the pattern. Every knitter is different. Some are loose knitters, some knit perfectly to gauge, and some are tight knitters. **Don't try to change your knitting style,** which will only make you unhappy and hurt your hands. **Change your needle size instead.** Continue swatching with larger or smaller needles until your gauge matches that which is called for in the pattern.

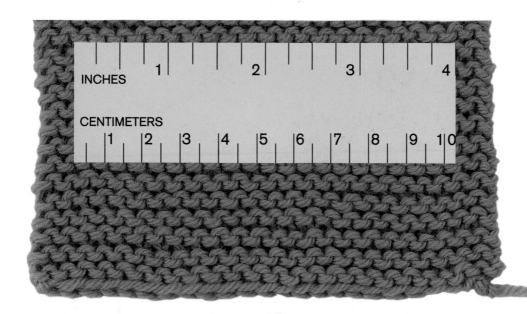

How to Knit a Garter Stitch Scarf

FINISHED DIMENSIONS

- 68" (173 cm) by 5" (13 cm)

1 Make a gauge swatch using the bulky weight yarn and US size 10 (6 mm) 9" (23 cm) single-pointed needles, the same yarn and needles as specified for the Garter Stitch Scarf on page 13. Cast on 16 stitches and work every row in knit stitch (garter stitch) until the length from the cast-on row is at least 4" (10 cm). Measure your swatch from side to side, or parallel to the needles, and do not measure the edge stitches. If necessary, switch to different size needles and knit a new swatch until you achieve the correct gauge.

2 **Cast on**
18 stitches.

3 **Row 1:**
Knit.

4 Repeat row 1 over and over until the length from the cast-on row is approximately 68" (173 cm) or desired length.

5 Bind off loosely and evenly.

6 Weave in loose ends to finish.

Loosely Knit Scarf

Believe it or not, the scarf shown in this project is the same width as the Garter Stitch Scarf on page 12. It's also made with the same number of stitches, yet it has a totally different look. The yarn used here is much lighter (thinner) than the chunky wool used in the Garter Stitch Scarf. Also, the needles used are much larger than the size specified on the yarn label. The result is a lacy scarf with gorgeous drape. In addition, the garter ridges are almost imperceptible. Instructions are on page 31.

WHAT YOU'LL LEARN...

- How to knit using a much larger needle than specified on yarn label

WHAT YOU'LL NEED...

YARN

- Super fine, multifiber yarn, approx. 160 yd (146 m)

  Shown: Filatura di Crosa *Gioiello* (30% kid mohair, 30% wool, 20% nylon, 10% cotton, 10% acrylic; 220 yd [201 m] per 1.75 oz [50 g] ball); color 44, 1 ball

NEEDLES AND NOTIONS

- US size 11 (8 mm) 9" (23 cm) single-pointed needles or size needed to achieve gauge

- Yarn needle for weaving in ends

GAUGE

- 14 sts = 4" (10 cm) in garter stitch

Skills and Useful Information

YARN LABEL INFORMATION

If you look at any yarn label it will tell you the suggested needle size and gauge. Generally the important information is shown using a little square that represents 4" (10 cm). The square shown below is typical and respresents the information you would find on worsted weight (medium) yarn.

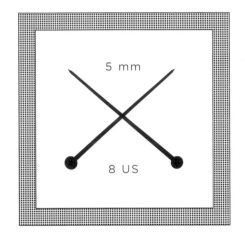

10 x 10 cm

4 x 4 inches

5 mm

8 US

28 R

20 S

The square itself represents a gauge swatch. Along the left side and top edge you'll find the measurement of the square, in both inches (4) and centimeters (10). Along the bottom of the square is the number 20 followed by S (or an R on European labels). That means that a 4" (10 cm) wide swatch of knitting should have 20 stitches. The number along the side, 28R, means that 4" (10 cm) should have 28 rows. The middle of the square shows a pair of crossed needles. The US size (8) is stated on the bottom and the metric size (5 mm) is above the needles. The gauge shown on the ball band is what is normally expected using that weight or thickness of yarn with the recommended needle size.

CHANGING NEEDLE SIZE TO VARY THE LOOK

The gauge as shown on a yarn label is what one would usually use to make a sweater. This would produce a knit piece of fabric that is of medium density that isn't stiff. There is no rule that says you have to use the needle that is suggested on the ball band. If you're making something like a coin purse or a pillow then perhaps you'll want to use a smaller needle to create a denser fabric with smaller stitches. On the other hand, you can make some beautiful and lacey sweaters and scarves if you use a needle that is larger or even much larger

US size 4 (3.5 mm)　　　　US size 8 (5 mm)　　　　US size 13 (9 mm)

than that specified on the ball band. Also, with larger stitches the knit fabric will have more drape.

The three swatches at left were made with the same yarn used in the Loosely Knit Scarf project that follows. These are the actual swatches I made when I was deciding which needle to specify for the pattern. The swatches were made using three different size needles, US size 4 (3.5 mm), US size 8 (5 mm), and US size 13 (9 mm). The respective width measurements are 4½" (11.5 cm), 6¼" (16 cm), and 9" (23 cm). You can easily see the variances in the density of the knit fabric.

How to Make a Loosely Knit Scarf

FINISHED DIMENSIONS

- 76" (193 cm) by 5¼" (13 cm)

You might notice when you make your scarf that the ends are wider compared to the center portion of the scarf (see below). This is normal and most prevalent when an item has been loosely knit like this scarf. A garter stitch scarf should be stored flat, not left hanging.

1 Make a gauge swatch using the yarn and needles specified. Cast on 16 stitches and work every row in knit stitch (garter stitch) until the length from the cast-on row is at least 4" (10 cm). Measure your swatch from side to side, or parallel to the needles, and do not measure the edge stitches. If necessary, switch to different size needles and knit a new swatch until you achieve the correct gauge.

2 **Cast on** 18 stitches.

3 **Row 1:** Knit.

4 Repeat row 1 over and over until the length from the cast-on row is approximately 76" (193 cm) or desired length.

5 Bind off loosely and evenly. Weave in loose ends to finish.

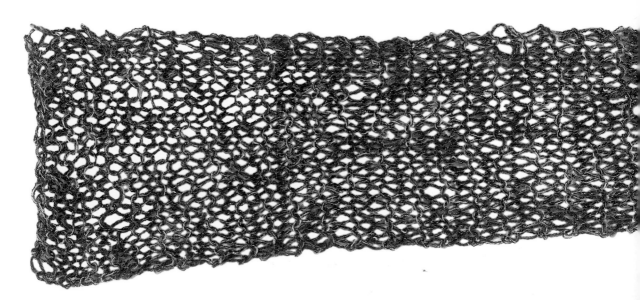

Scarf Knit with Two Yarns

This scarf is made by combining a bumpy bouclé yarn with a short eyelash/novelty yarn. The novelty yarn has a hint of metallic, which adds some intriguing sparkle to the boucle yarn. Instructions are on page 38.

WHAT YOU'LL LEARN . . . .

- How to knit with two yarns at the same time
- How to add a fringe to a scarf

WHAT YOU'LL NEED . . . .

YARN

- Yarn A: bulky weight boucle yarn, approx. 130 yd (119 m)

  Shown: Sublime *Wooly Merino* (96% merino wool, 4% nylon; 96 yd [88 m] per 1.75 oz [50 g] ball); blue, color 180, 2 balls

- Yarn B: light weight novelty yarn, approx. 130 yd (119 m)

  Shown: Crystal Palace Yarns, *Little Flowers* (96% nylon, 4% metallic fiber; 130 yd [119 m] per 1.75 oz [50 g] ball); Berry Compote, color 2233, 1 ball

NEEDLES AND NOTIONS

- US size 11 (8 mm) 9" (23 cm) single-pointed needles or size needed to achieve gauge
- Yarn needle for weaving in ends
- Crochet hook, US size K-10½ (6. 5mm)
- Pins for marking placement of fringe

GAUGE

- 9 sts = 4" (10 cm) in stockinette stitch

Skills and Useful Information

Once you've mastered the basic knit stitch, a whole world of knitting exploration will be opened. Not only can you vary the gauge (how loose or tight the stitches are) you can also change the look of a scarf by knitting with two or more yarns together at the same time.

COMBINING YARN

Yarn is typically classified by the thickness or diameter of the strand and this classification is commonly referred to weight. Don't confuse the weight in terms of thickness compared to the total actual weight of the yarn ball or skein (usually 1.75 oz [50 g] or 3.5 oz [100 g]). The thickness, or weight, of yarn translates into how many stitches can be fit into an inch of knitting, and it also dictates how big the diameter of the needle shank should be.

You will often hear a yarn's weight referred to using traditional, somewhat archaic terminology such as fingering, sport, worsted, and so on. In the United States, the Craft Yarn Council has encouraged the use of a uniform standard of yarn measurement. Knitters have remained somewhat stubborn and often continue to use the traditional names. The most important information you need to know about a yarn's weight is **stitches per inch.**

As you gain experience as a knitter you will become familiar with the best use for a particular weight of yarn. The table below gives information about current yarn classifications.

When two or more strands of yarn are combined the resulting yarn is, obviously, thicker. It helps to have an idea of the approximate weight of common combinations so you have a ballpark idea of what needle to use. Refer to the table at right for some common combinations.

The best combinations of yarn are those that highlight differences while still complementing one another. Two examples are shown opposite.

Mohair is a great addition to smooth yarn, giving it some fuzz and softness, but it's most effectively used when the two colors are coordinated (A).

On the other hand, when combining two yarns of similar texture, contrasting colors can work

Craft Yarn Council Designation	Traditional Name	Traditional Uses	Stitches per inch	US needle size
Lace 1	Lace	Lace	8 to 10	000 to 1
Super Fine 2	Fingering	Sock, baby	7 to 8	0 to 3
Fine 3	Sport	Baby, colorwork	6	3 to 5
Light 4	DK (Double Knitting)	Indoor garments, colorwork, children	5½	5 to 7
Medium 5	Worsted	All types of garments; most commonyarn weight	5	7 to 9
	Aran	Fisherman cable sweaters	4 to 4½	8 to 10
Bulky 6	Chunky	Outdoor garments	3½	9 to 11
Super Bulky 7	Bulky	Coat sweaters, hats, mittens	2 to 2½	11 and larger

Yarns to Combine	Equivalent Weight of Combined Yarn	Suggested US Needle Size for Combined Yarn
2 strands of fingering (super fine)	1 strand of DK (light)	5 to 7
1 strand of fingering (super fine) and 1 strand of sport (fine)	1 strand of worsted (medium)	7 to 9
2 strands of worsted (medium)	1 strand of chunky (bulky)	9 to 11
1 strand of worsted (medium) and 1 strand of chunky (bulky)	1 strand of bulky (super bulky)	11 and larger

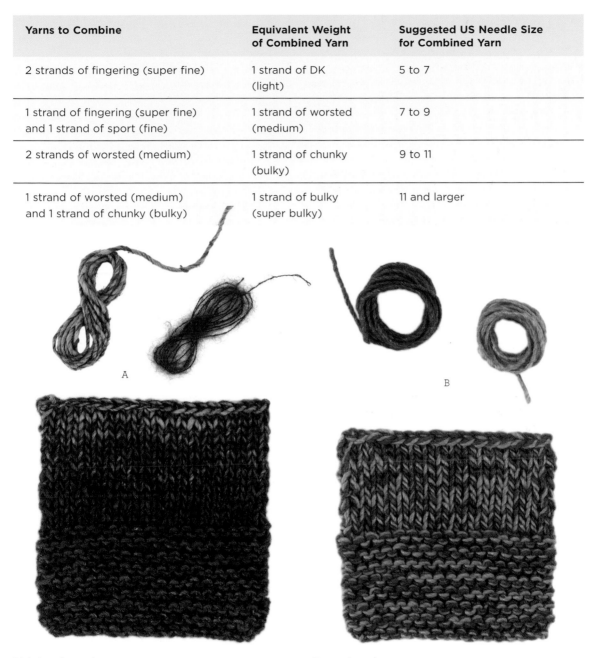

Mohair and smooth yarn

Contrasting colors

beautifully. Also, if you fall in love with a yarn that seems too fine for a scarf, then combine two strands to make a chunkier yarn (B).

Explore your creativity using the huge range of yarns available at your LYS or craft store. Be brave! Put some yarns together and make a swatch to explore what combinations of texture and color you like. If the result isn't what you expected, take joy in the learning process and try a different combination. But save the yarn that "didn't make the cut"; another yarn will make the perfect partner sometime in the future.

KNITTING WITH TWO YARNS HELD TOGETHER

Pull a length of yarn from each ball that is long enough to cast on the desired number of stitches. For a scarf, about 3 ft (0.92 m) is usually more than enough. Line up the ends and then draw the tails through your fingers a few times so the yarns cling to each other.

1 Pinch the two yarns together and form a slip knot with both yarns. Your "yarn" now consists of one strand each of two different yarns.

2 Cast on the desired number of stitches, always using both strands of yarn together and treating them as if they were one strand.

3 When the right needle enters the loop of the stitch on the left needle it needs to go through both strands. Likewise, when wrapping the yarn around the right needle to make a stitch both strands should be wrapped together.

4 You will most likely be combining yarns that are packaged in different lengths and will run out of one yarn before the other. Follow the directions on page 21 for joining new yarn.

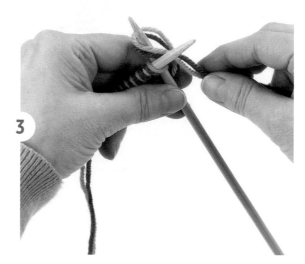

FRINGE

The contrasting look and texture of fringe can add a lot of drama to a scarf. The fringe can be simple, made from the same yarn as the scarf, or it can be made using a completely different yarn in a contrasting color. The strands of yarn in the fringe can be consistent from one fringe section to the next, or you can mix up the strands. It's all up to you. If you plan to make the fringe using the same yarn as knit in the scarf, then plan ahead and set some yarn aside for the fringe before you start knitting.

1

4A

4B

2

3

When deciding on what yarns and how many strands to put in the fringe, remember that the pieces will be folded in half after cutting. So, two cut pieces in a fringe section will actually make four ends.

1 Cut the fringe to twice the length desired plus 1" (2.5 cm). I often use a video dvd case: wrap the fringe around and around the desired number of times before cutting across the wraps on one end. Going around the long way makes a good fringe for a women's scarf and the short way is appropriate for children's and men's scarves.

2 Arrange the fringe pieces in bundles. The bundle will contain all the cut lengths for each fringe section. Fold the bundle in half.

3 Insert a crochet hook through the scarf on the edge where you want the fringe to be. Hook the fringe at the fold point and pull the fold through the scarf so that about half of the length is pulled through the scarf, forming a loop.

4 Reach through the loop with your fingers and pinch the cut ends, pulling them back through the loop (A). Gently pull the ends down until the loop tightens (B).

How to Knit a Scarf Made with Two Yarns

FINISHED DIMENSIONS

- 50" x 5¼" (127 x 13 cm) (without fringe)
- 64" x 5¼" (163 x 13 cm) (with fringe)

1 Before you begin knitting, cut and set aside approximately 10 yards (9 m) each of yarn A and yarn B for the fringe. With yarn A and yarn B held together, **cast on** 12 stitches.

2 Row 1: With yarn A and yarn B held together, knit every stitch to the end of the row.

3 Repeat row 1 until the scarf is 50" (127 cm) or the desired length. Bind off all stitches loosely and evenly. Weave in loose ends to finish.

4

5

MAKE THE FRINGE

4 Cut 24 pieces of yarn A and 24 pieces of yarn B to a length of 14" (36 cm). Arrange 12 fringe bundles, each with two pieces of yarn A and two pieces of yarn B. Confirm fringe length.

5 Measure the end of the scarf and mark the fringe locations approximately 1" (2.5 cm) apart starting and ending at each corner. There will be a total of six fringe sections.

6 Using the crochet hook and following the general directions on page 37, attach one fringe section to each point marked by the pin.

7 If desired, trim the fringe to an even length using scissors or a rotary cutter.

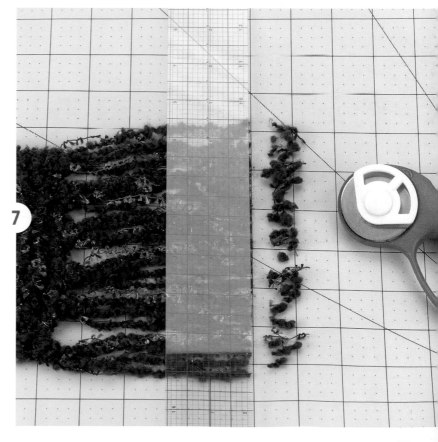

7

Texture

The primary means of creating texture in knitting is combining knit stitches with purl stitches. Once you've mastered purling, a huge variety of stitches will open up for you. In this chapter you'll learn just a few: stockinette stitch, reverse stockinette stitch, seed stitch, and rib. Another fascinating method for adding texture to knitting is the cable, which crosses one column of stitches over another. The simple cable taught in this chapter will give you a mere glimpse into the huge array of cable stitches that are used in knitting.

Baby Blocks Blanket

A baby blanket made with blocks of stockinette stitch and reverse stockinette stitch is a great project for you to learn and practice a new skill: purling. The blanket is a perfect size for baby to bring along in a car seat or stroller. Instructions begin on page 51.

WHAT YOU'LL LEARN

- How to purl
- How to use cable cast-on
- How to use a circular needle to knit back and forth
- How to use stitch markers
- How to modify a pattern to make the item bigger or smaller
- How to alternate between knit and purl in the same row
- How to read a stitch pattern with repeats
- How to combine garter stitch, stockinette stitch, and reverse stockinette stitch in a block pattern
- How to damp block an item

WHAT YOU'LL NEED

YARN

- Medium weight smooth yarn, approx. 715 yd (654 m). Since this is a baby blanket, consider using a yarn that is washable, such as a wool and acrylic blend or washable wool.

  Shown: Berroco *Comfort* (50% super fine nylon, 50% super fine acrylic; 210 yd [192 m] per 3.5 oz [100 g] skein); turquoise, color 9733, 4 skeins

NEEDLES AND NOTIONS

- US size 7 (4.5 mm) circular needle at least 24" (61 cm) long or size needed to achieve gauge. The circular needle is necessary to accommodate the large number of stitches. You will be knitting back and forth on the circular needle.
- Yarn needle for weaving in ends
- Stitch markers
- Rust-proof pins for blocking

EQUIPMENT

- Washing machine
- Towels

GAUGE

- 20 sts = 4" (10 cm) in stockinette stitch

Skills and Useful Information

So far you've learned how to make a simple knit scarf using **cast-on**, **knit**, and **bind-off**. There's one more essential skill to add—**the purl stitch**.

Practice Swatch: Purl (P, p)

Make a practice swatch using worsted weight yarn and US size 8 (5 mm) 9" (23 cm) single-pointed needles. (see pages 6–9 for more information about materials and needles).

1. Begin the practice swatch by **casting on** 25 stitches and knitting 1 row.

2. Hold the needles as you would for knitting but with the working yarn in front. The needle with the stitches on it will be in your left hand and the empty needle in your right hand. Working from the back to the front, insert the right needle into the first stitch on the left needle (the one closest to the tip), going through the loop just above the bump. (Some knitters find it easier to envision this step as inserting the needle from the right to the left.)

3. Use the fingers of your left hand to hold the needles so they form an X (the right needle will be in front).

4. Pick up the working yarn with your right hand and wrap it around the right-hand needle in a counterclockwise direction. Later you will learn some special techniques for grasping the working yarn. For now, simply hold the working yarn between the thumb and forefinger of your right hand when called for.

5. Holding the working yarn (with a bit of tension) and the right needle together, dip the needle down to the left and then <u>away</u> from you, drawing the working yarn through the first stitch on the left needle. The right needle will now be to back of the left needle with a new loop of yarn on it.

6. Slide the right needle to the right and off the end of the left needle, taking the newly formed stitch off the left needle. The original stitch will come with it. One purl stitch has been completed. Work several more rows of purl stitch until you feel comfortable with the movements.

Practice Swatch: Alternating Knit Rows and Purl Rows to Make Stockinette Stitch (St st)

Stockinette stitch is created when knit rows are alternated with purl rows. Continue on the purl practice swatch, but first mark one side with a safety pin or locking stitch marker. This will be the side on which knit rows are made; the side without the marker will be for purl rows.

Work two rows as follows:

Row 1 (with marker): Knit all stitches.

Row 2: Purl all stitches.

Continue, repeating rows 1 and 2 over and over. Practice until you feel completely comfortable with stockinette stitch. Bind off.

The Difference Between a Knit Stitch and a Purl Stitch

Take a look at the swatch you just made and observe how the knit stitches and purl stitches have unique characteristics.

The knit stitches (on the side of the swatch with the marker) form flat, vertical "V"s on the side facing you (1).

Purl stitches form horizontal bars or bumps on the side facing you (2).

The knit stitch and the purl stitch are the alter egos of each other. The wrong side of the knit stitch looks like purl and the wrong side of purl looks like knit. The bumpy, purl side of stockinette stitch is called **reverse stockinette stitch** (rev St st).

SWITCHING BETWEEN KNIT STITCH AND PURL STITCH IN THE SAME ROW

Texture stitches will most often require you to switch between a knit stitch and a purl stitch or a combination of stitches in the same row. When you are making a knit stitch, the yarn is in back of the needle; for a purl stitch the yarn is in front of the needle. When switching between a knit stitch and a purl stitch it is necessary to move the yarn back and forth between the needles. It's very important that the yarn goes between the needles when moving back and forth, not over or around them.

Stockinette Stitch Needs a Partner

You will rarely see stockinette stitch used as the only stitch in a scarf. The edges of stockinette stitch curl, and a scarf made only from this stitch will turn in upon itself to form a long tube. To avoid this, you must use some other stitch to make the top, bottom, and sides of the knitting. Take the time now to make a practice swatch that will demonstrate how to control the edge curl of stockinette stitch.

Practice Swatch:
Switching Between Knit and Purl in the Same Row

Practice switching between knit and purl on the same row by making a practice swatch using worsted weight yarn and US size 8 (5 mm) 9″ (23 cm) single-pointed needles. (See pages 6–9 for more information about materials and needles.)

1. Begin the practice swatch by **casting on**
   24 stitches.

Rows 1 to 6: Knit

2. Now you will make the main area of the swatch by repeating two rows over and over. The swatch will have a border of garter stitch (knit on both sides) with a middle section of stockinette stitch (knit 1 row, purl 1 row). Before beginning theses rows, read the section above about switching between knit stitch and purl stitch.

Row 7: Knit 4, move yarn between the needles to the front, purl 16, move yarn between the needles to the back, knit 4

Row 8: Knit

Repeat rows 7 and 8 until the swatch is almost square or until you've reached the desired length.

To finish, work six additional rows in garter stitch:

3. **Rows 9 to 14:** Knit

   Bind off.

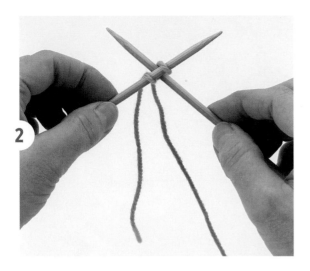

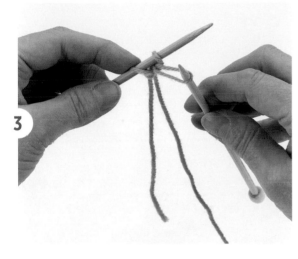

CABLE CAST-ON

The baby blanket pattern requires that you cast on 144 stitches. It's frustrating to get almost finished with casting on using the long-tail method, only to discover that your tail is too short to complete all the required stitches and you need to start over. The cable cast-on can be used in place of a standard long-tail cast-on. It's also very useful for adding stitches at the beginning of an existing row. When used for the original cast-on it requires only a short tail, so you don't need to worry about estimating the length of the tail incorrectly.

1 Begin by making a slip knot (page 14), leaving a tail about 8" (20 cm) long. Place the right needle into the loop made by the slip knot and wrap the yarn around as if you were making a knit stitch. Instead of leaving this stitch on the right needle, place it on the left needle.

2 Insert the right needle into space between the first and second stitch on the left needle.

3 Wrap the yarn around the right needle and pull a loop through to the front as if you were knitting a stitch.

4 Place this new loop back onto the left needle.

Repeat steps 2, 3, and 4 until the desired number of stitches has been added. It is not necessary to switch the needle to the left hand after the cast-on row. It is already oriented to begin the first row of knitting.

KNITTING FLAT ITEMS
USING A CIRCULAR NEEDLE

Circular needles are most often used for knitting a cylinder, such as a sweater body or a hat, but they are also quite useful when the width of an item is much too large to fit on a straight needle, even a long one. When the number of stitches exceeds the width of a straight needle, the solution is to knit back and forth on a circular needle. Think of the circular needle as two regular (single-pointed) needles that have been tied together with a string.

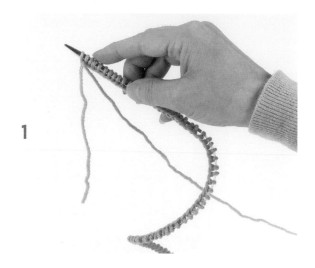

1 To cast on using the long-tail method, hold the needle in your right hand as usual. As you cast on more and more stitches, they will slide off the needle and onto the cable (the string).

2 When you finish casting on transfer the needle to your left hand with the needle tip pointing to the right. With your right hand, pick up the other end of the needle. Just ignore the cable and start knitting as always.

3 As with the cast-on row, the stitches will move off the right needle and on to the cable as you knit across the row.

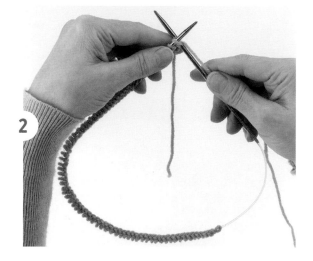

4 When you finish the row, all of the stitches will have been transferred to the right needle. Switch again, putting the needle that's in your right hand into your left hand with the needle tip pointing to the right. Pick up the empty side of the needle and start the next row.

Casting on to a circular needle using the cable cast-on method is very similar except all the stitches will be cast on to the left needle and you will be using the right needle to make the cast-on loops. It is not necessary to switch the needle to the left hand after the cast-on row. It is already oriented to begin the first row of knitting.

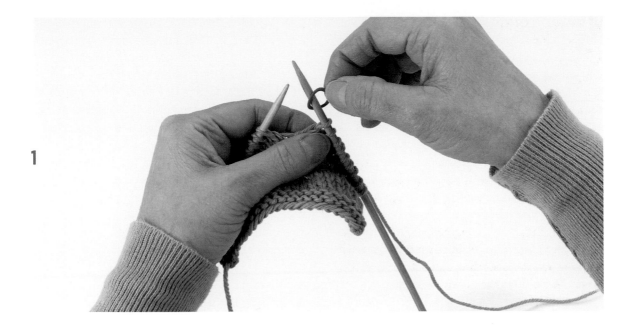

1

2

STITCH MARKERS
Place Marker (pm)
Slip Marker (sm)
Remove Marker (rm)

Stitch markers can be very helpful in a pattern like this one to mark the beginning and end of a set of stitches. In this pattern each 12-stitch block is enclosed by markers.

1 To place a marker (pm) simply slip it on to the right needle at the point indicated in the pattern.

2 When you reach a marker while knitting a row, slip it from the left needle to the right needle (sm) and continue with the next repeat.

3 When it's time to remove the marker (rm), simply knit the stitch to the right of the marker, take the marker off the left needle and set aside, then continue knitting without the marker.

DAMP BLOCKING

Most knit items you make will need to be blocked. The process of blocking uses steam or moisture to even out and relax the stitches, smooth out the knit fabric, and straighten the edges. To a certain degree blocking can be used to make a piece of knitting conform to the intended shape, such as square or an angle in a garment piece such as a sleeve. Blocking can make an item somewhat bigger if desired but is not effective in making an item smaller. Certain types of knitting such as lace require blocking in order to make the stitches lie flat.

If the item you've made is delicate or the yarn contains nylon, then it's a good candidate for damp blocking. This method is also effective for an item that is too big for steaming on your ironing board.

Block the item in a sandwich of damp towels that have been immersed in water in your washer and then spun dry. Start by placing a damp towel on a blocking board, carpeted floor, or bed mattress. The towel should be wider and longer than the item you will be blocking; if necessary use more than one towel. Lay the item to be blocked on top of the wet towel and smooth it into shape. Use rustproof T-pins to pin the item to the blocking surface beginning with the corners. Use a tape measure to make sure the width and length are consistent or the item matches the dimensions and shape specified in the pattern. Continue by pinning all the edges at frequent intervals. Cover the entire item with a second damp towel. Leave the towels in place until the item is completely dry.

READING PATTERNS

Brackets [ ] are often used in patterns as a shorthand way of expressing a repeated instruction. The brackets enclose a set of instructions such as [k12, p12] followed by the number of repeats required, such as 3 times.

So, if you see the direction [k12, p12] 3 times, then you would k12, p12, k12, p12, k12, p12.

HEIGHT AND WIDTH DIFFERENCES OF KNIT STITCHES

A knit stitch is wider than it is tall. This presents some challenges when attempting to knit blocks. In order to achieve a square shape there must be more rows (vertically) than stitches (horizontally) in a block. You'll see this in the baby blanket pattern. Each block is 12 stitches wide, but 18 rows are worked in order to achieve a square shape for each of the blocks. Keep this in mind when you start creating designs of your own.

MODIFYING THE PATTERN TO BE BIGGER OR SMALLER

If you look in any stitch guide book it will tell you that a stitch pattern is a multiple of a given number of stitches. That is true of the blocks pattern used to make this blanket. Each block is 12 stitches wide and there are eleven blocks (132 stitches). In addition, there are 6 edge stitches (worked in garter stitch – all knit) on either side, an additional 12 stitches for a total of 144 stitches in the pattern. As you can see, this pattern is a multiple of 12 stitches. If you want to make the blanket wider, then add stitches in a multiple of 12; likewise if you want it to be narrower, then subtract stitches in a multiple of 12. For instance, if you want to add two extra blocks to the width (2 × 12), then you would cast on 168 stitches (144 + 24).

In addition to a pattern repeat worked into the number of stitches, a pattern usually has a row repeat as well. This pattern is worked for 18 rows, at which point the stockinette stitch and reverse stockinette stitch sections are switched for another 18 rows. So, the pattern has a 36-row repeat for two complete sets of alternating blocks. However if you only want to add one additional set of blocks you would add a single set of 18 rows.

How to Knit the Baby Blocks Blanket

FINISHED DIMENSIONS

- 28½" (72 cm) by 28½" (72 cm)

1 **Cast on** stitches and make blanket edging placing markers on final row of edging.

Cast on 144 sts using the cable cast-on method.

Rows 1 to 10: Knit.

Row 11: K6, [pm, k12] repeat 11 times, pm, k6.

2 Make first set of blocks.

Row 1: K6, [sm, k12, p12] 5 times, sm, k12, sm, k6.

Row 2: K6, [sm, p12, k12] 5 times, sm, p12, sm, k6.

Rows 3 to 18: Repeat rows 1 and 2 eight more times.

3 Make second set of blocks.

Row 19: K6, [sm, p12, k12] 5 times, sm, p12, sm, k6.

Row 20: K6, [sm, k12, p12] 5 times, sm, k12, sm, k6.

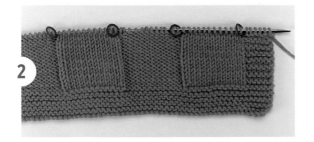

Rows 21 to 36: Repeat rows 19 and 20 eight more times.

4 Continue knitting until 11 sets of blocks are completed. You can now see how the two groups of 18 rows (36 rows total) form two sets of blocks made from contrasting stockinette stitch and reverse stockinet stitch. The 36-row repeat is worked four more times and then the first 18 rows are repeated once.

Rows 37 to 180: Repeat rows 1 to 36 four more times.

Rows 181 to 198: Repeat rows 1 to 18 once.

5 Remove stitch markers and make edging.

Row 1: Knit, removing stitch markers as you come to them.

Rows 2 to 11: Knit.

6 Bind off loosely and evenly. Cut yarn, leaving a tail at least 8" (20 cm) long.

7 Finishing: weave in all ends and damp block if desired.

Seed Stitch Table Runner

Seed stitch is one of the most useful and versatile stitches available to knitters. The edges don't curl, making it a perfect stitch for scarves and blankets. The rhythmic repetition of the bumps is ideal for accentuating variegated yarns, but it adds interest to solid-colored pieces as well. Seed stitch also drapes beautifully. Seed stitch works well when using needles larger than is typical for the weight of yarn, making it an excellent way to get more knit area from less yarn and allowing you to use a yarn that you might otherwise think twice about buying because of its price but can't resist because of its beauty. Instructions for the table runner are on page 59.

WHAT YOU'LL LEARN

- How knit seed stitch
- How to bind off stitches in pattern
- How to make a seed stitch table runner
- How to modify the pattern for a scarf
- English and Continental methods of knitting
- How to knit ribbing

WHAT YOU'LL NEED

YARN

- Super bulky weight smooth, variegated yarn, approx. 200 yd (183 m)

  Shown: Berroco *Borealis* (60% acrylic, 40% wool; 108yd [100 m] per 3.5 oz [100 g] skein); Olafsvik, color 5059, 2 skeins

NEEDLES AND NOTIONS

- US size 13 (9 mm) 9" (23 cm) single-pointed needles or size needed to achieve gauge
- Yarn needle for weaving in ends

GAUGE

- 10 sts = 4" (10 cm) in seed stitch stitch

Skills and Useful Information

HOW TO HOLD THE YARN AND NEEDLES—ENGLISH OR CONTINENTAL METHOD

There are as many ways to hold knitting needles and tension the yarn as there are cultures. However, there are two predominant methods, and they depend on which hand holds the working yarn; right hand for the English method and left hand for the Continental method. The English method is sometimes referred to as "throwing" and the Continental method is sometimes referred to as "picking." The hand you use to hold the yarn is not determined by which is your dominant hand. It's a matter of what makes you feel more comfortable, what you've been exposed to (how did your mom or aunt knit) and the specific task you are undertaking.

Generally speaking, the yarn is intertwined through the fingers and often wrapped around the little finger. You can see the English method below and the Continental method above on the left. The act of twining the yarn through the fingers keeps it organized, ready at hand, and gives it a bit of tension. If you learn to do this you will be able to knit much faster than when you pick up the yarn to wrap it for each individual stitch. You don't have to twine the yarn the same way as shown; if a different method works better for you then use it.

Continental method

READING PATTERNS

You will find a paired asterisk symbol (*) used in the patterns which indicates a repeat of the directions found between the asterisks (* *). Generally, directions between asterisks such as *K2, p2* are repeated over and over to the end of the row or until a specified number of stitches remain.

English method

Practice Swatch: English and Continental Methods

Familiarize yourself with the two methods of knitting by making a practice swatch using worsted weight yarn and US size 8 (5 mm) 9" (23 cm) single-pointed needles (see pages 6–9 for more information about materials and needles).

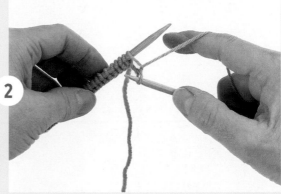

Knitting Using the English Method

All of the instruction to this point has been taught using the English method except that the yarn wasn't twined in the fingers; it was pinched between the thumb and forefinger.

With the English method it helps to insert the needle into the right stitch first and hold both needles with your left hand as you twine the yarn around your right fingers and prepare to knit or purl.

1. **Cast on** 25 stitches. With the yarn at the back of the needle, twine the yarn as shown (opposite, bottom), and move your whole hand to wrap or "throw" the yarn around the needle to make the loop for the stitch.

2. Instead of holding the yarn along with the needle to provide tension, allow the yarn to rest over the forefinger when pulling the new loop through the old stitch.

   Work a few rows on your swatch in knit stitch using the English method.

Purling Using the English Method

3. Purling using the English method is very similar to knitting. Wrap the yarn through your fingers in the same manner but keep the yarn in front of the needles. Work a few rows on your swatch in purl stitch using the English method.

(continued)

Knitting Using the Continental Method

The Continental method will feel quite different to you at first if you've only used the English method. Many knitters find this method to be much faster but only after some practice.

1. To start, twine the yarn through the fingers of your left hand as shown on page 54, top. The working yarn should drape over the left forefinger with some tension. The yarn is held behind and no more than 1" (2.5 cm) above the left needle.

2. Insert the right needle into the first stitch on the left needle from front to back. Catch or "pick" a loop for the new stitch by moving the right needle over and then under the working yarn.

3. Pull this new loop through the stitch on the left needle and onto the right needle just like the English method. Work a few rows on your swatch in knit stitch using the Continental method.

Purling Using the Continental Method

1. Twine the yarn around the fingers of the left hand as with knitting and hold the working yarn to the front of the needles.

2. Insert the right needle into the first stitch on the left needle from back to front. Cock your right forefinger down behind the right needle in order to lay the working yarn over and then behind the right needle.

3. Keeping tension on the loop, move the right needle to the back, and pull the new loop through the old stitch onto the right needle just like the English method. Work a few rows on your Swatch in purl stitch using the Continental method.

  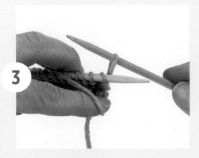

SEED STITCH

In the first section of this chapter you learned how to combine large blocks of similar stitches. Many texture stitches will require you to switch between knit and purl every 1 or 2 stitches. One of those stitches is seed stitch, which is knit 1 stitch, purl 1 stitch alternating across the row. The important thing to remember about switching between knits and purls on the same row is to **move the yarn between the needles to the front for a purl stitch and between the needles to the back for a knit stitch.**

Take a moment to think about how you worked the seed stitch, remembering that a knit stitch looks like a "V" and a purl stitch looks like a bump. When working in seed stitch you do the opposite of what the stitch on the left needle looks like. If you see a bump right under the needle, then knit the stitch. Or, if you see a "V" under the needle, then purl the stitch.

knit this stitch

purl this stitch

TIP When making an item using seed stitch it's easier to cast on an odd number of stitches. That way every row begins and ends with a knit stitch and you don't have to worry about what row you're on.

Practice Swatch: Seed Stitch

Practice seed stitch by making a practice swatch using worsted weight yarn and US size 8 (5 mm) 9" (23 cm) single-pointed needles (see page 6-9 for more information about materials and needles).

Cast on 21 stitches.

1. **Row 1:** K1, move yarn to back of needle, *p1, move yarn to front of needle, k1, move yarn to back of needle*; repeat from * to * to end of row.

Continue repeating row 1 until you are completely comfortable with the seed stitch. Bind off in pattern following the directions on page 58.

RIBBING

Ribbing and seed stitch have the same foundation, that is, stitches are knit and purled across the row. The difference is that seed stitch alternates knit stitches vertically against purl stitches, thus creating a checkerboard pattern. In ribbing, the **same** stitches line up in vertical columns, knit stitches directly above knit stitches and purl stitches directly above purl stitches. You won't use ribbing until later in the book but it's taught here because of its close resemblance to seed stitch.

Ribbing is frequently used in knitting. It has a great deal of elasticity, which allows it to contract, making it an ideal stitch for waistlines and cuffs on sweaters or the brim of a hat. In order to make it fit more closely, ribbing is often worked in a needle that is smaller than the

body of the garment. Sometimes ribbing is referred to as 2 × 2 or 3 × 3, etc. These numbers specify the distribution of knits and purls in each ribbing repeat. In other words, 2 × 2 would be a knit 2, purl 2 ribbing.

Compare the technique for making ribbing to that for making seed stitch. In seed stitch you work the stitch the opposite way it presents itself. For instance, if you see a purl bump under the needle, then you knit the stitch. **Ribbing is the opposite.** You always work the stitch in the same manner it presents itself. If you see the "V" of a knit stitch, then work the new stitch in knit; if you see the bump of a purl, then work the new stitch in purl.

Do not steam block ribbing. Once steam blocked, ribbing will remain stretched out. The photo at left shows a swatch that has been steam blocked open so that the details of the ribs can be seen.

BINDING OFF IN PATTERN

Sometimes when you have made an item that has a pattern stitch such as ribbing or seed stitch all the way to the edge, the

Practice Swatch: Ribbing

Learn more about the different types of ribbing by making a practice swatch using worsted weight yarn and US size 8 (5 mm) 9″ (23 cm) single-pointed needles (see pages 6–9 for more information about materials and needles).

Cast on 24 stitches. Learn how to knit a variety of rib stitches by working the following rows:

Rows 1 to 8 (1 x 1 rib): *K1, p1*; repeat from * to * to end of row.

Rows 9 to 16 (2 x 2 rib): *K2, p2*; repeat from * to * to end of row.

Rows 17 to 24 (3 x 3 rib): *K3, p3*; repeat from * to * to end of row.

Rows 25 to 36 (4 x 4 rib): *K4, p4*; repeat from * to * to end of row.

Bind off in pattern following the directions above.

directions might call for binding off in pattern. This just means that you should maintain the same pattern stitch (for instance *k1, p1*) in the bind-off row as was used in the preceding rows. Maintain the knit or purl pattern as specified by the directions but work the bind-off on the right needle, continuing to pass the first stitch over the second stitch on the right needle. For more detailed information see step 3 in the pattern below.

MODIFYING THE PATTERN TO MAKE A SCARF

The pattern presented below makes a table runner that is 11½" (29 cm) wide by 38" (97 cm) long. The design can easily be modified to make a scarf by casting on fewer stitches and making a narrower but longer piece. Remember, seed stitch is easiest to knit with an odd number of stitches so that you don't need to remember whether you're on the right side or wrong side. If you work seed stitch with an odd number of stitches, then every row is worked identically.

To make a scarf instead, cast on 17 stitches. Follow the stitch pattern until there is just enough yarn to bind off or you have reached the desired length. If you use the same amount of yarn as the table runner you should get a scarf that is about 6¾" (17 cm) by 65" (165 cm), provided you are knitting at the same gauge as specified.

How to Knit the Seed Stitch Table Runner

FINISHED DIMENSIONS

- 11½" (29 cm) wide by 38" (97 cm) long

1 **Cast on** 29 stitches.

2 **Row 1:** *K1, p1*; repeat from * to * to end of row.

Repeat row 1 until the length from the cast-on edge is approximately 38" (97 cm) or the desired length. Be sure to leave at least 2 yds (1.8 m) for binding off.

3 Bind off stitches in pattern as follows:

Step 1: K1.

Step 2: P1.

Step 3: Pass first stitch on right needle over second stitch and off the end of the needle (one stitch has been bound off).

Step 4: K1.

Step 5: Pass first stitch on right needle over second stitch and off the end of the needle (one stitch has been bound off).

Repeat bind off steps 2 to 5 until 1 stitch remains on needle. Cut yarn leaving a tail at least 8" (20 cm) long and pull through last stitch, tighten to secure.

4 To finish, weave in ends. Damp block or steam block if the yarn you've chosen does not contain acrylic or nylon. See page 67 for more information on steam blocking.

Cabled Smart Phone Case

A small case for a smart phone is a great project for learning to knit cables. The cables give the knit fabric a density that makes a nice protective cover for your phone. The pattern (page 68) is sized for a phone that is 10½" (26.5 cm) in circumference lengthwise and 6" (15 cm) in circumference widthwise. Directions are given on page 67 for changing the pattern to fit other dimensions.

WHAT YOU'LL LEARN..

- How to increase and decrease stitches using kf&b and k2tog
- How to make right-crossing and left-crossing cables

- How to make a cabled phone cover
- How to modify the pattern to fit your phone
- How to steam block

WHAT YOU'LL NEED..

YARN

- Medium weight, smooth yarn, approx. 57 yd (52 m)

  Shown: Plymouth Yarn *Worsted Merino Superwash* (100% superwash merino wool; 218 yd [200 m] per 3.5 oz [100 g] ball); color 3, 1 skein

NEEDLES AND NOTIONS

- US size 6 (4 mm) 9" (23 cm) single-pointed needle or size needed to achieve gauge
- Cable needle
- Yarn needle for weaving in ends
- Rust-proof pins for blocking
- Sewing thread to match yarn color
- Sewing needle
- Velcro sew-in coins or dots

EQUIPMENT

- Iron
- Ironing board

GAUGE

- 20 sts = 4" (10 cm) in stockinette stitch
- 25 sts = 4" (10 cm) in cable pattern (Cable patterns contract the knitting from side to side.)

Note: The gauge swatch can be worked using stockinette stitch.

Skills and Useful Information

CABLES

One of the most dramatic ways to add texture to a knit item is with cables. Many knitters are intimidated by cables but they need not be. Quite simply, a cable is created by knitting groups of stitches out of order. When knitting across the row, a group of stitches is put on hold using a short needle called a cable needle. The stitches are kept out of the way while the next group of stitches is knit from left needle. Next, the out-of-order stitches from the cable needle are worked, which reverses the order of the two groups of stitches.

Cables are normally worked on a background of reverse stockinette stitch or garter stitch, sometimes even seed stitch. This is done to accentuate the knit stitches in the cable. A cable is usually crossed in the same interval of rows as the number of stitches. So, a 6-stitch cable would be crossed every 6 rows.

Where the stitches are kept while on hold determines the direction that the cable crosses. If the stitches are held on the cable needle in front of the knitting while working the out-of-order stitches, then the cable will cross to left (1). Stitches held on the cable needle to the back of the knitting will create a right-crossing cable (2).

Cables have their own shorthand terms used to define their characteristics. The two cables used in this pattern are 6-st RKC and 6-st LKC. The stitch count refers to how many stitches in total are in the cable. This number is divided in half: 3 stitches cross one way and 3 the other way. Next comes the letter R or L, indicating the direction the cable crosses—right or left. K means that the stitches being crossed are knit (rather than purled), and C simply stands for cross. In other books you may find different terminology to mean the same thing such as C6B (same as 6-st RKC) or C6F (same as 6-st LKC).

Left knit cross (LKC)

Right knit cross (RKC)

Six-Stitch Left Knit Cross (6-st LKC)

1 Work the stitches preceding the cable; if necessary, move the yarn to the back of the needles. Slip the next 3 stitches from the left needle on to the cable needle (insert the cable needle into the stitches as if you were getting ready to purl them).

2 Drop the cable needle and let it hang loosely at the front of the knitting.

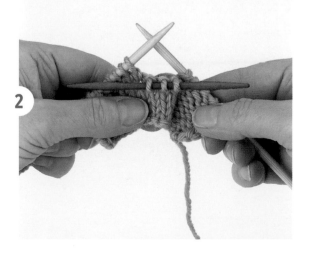

3 Working behind the cable needle, knit the next 3 stitches on the left needle.

4 Slide the held stitches to the right side of the cable needle and knit them using the right needle. The cable is complete. Work the stitches after the cable according to the pattern.

5 When you work the wrong side, you don't need to do anything special with the cable stitches since they have already been crossed. The cable stitches will be a little crowded, but simply knit or purl them according to the pattern.

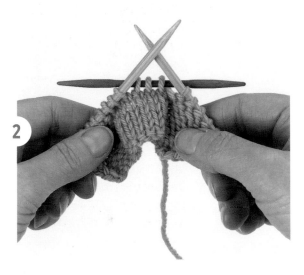

Six-Stitch Right Knit Cross (6-st RKC)

1 The right knit cross is worked in a similar manner to the left cross. Reach in from behind the knitting needles and slip the next 3 stitches on to the cable needle (insert the cable needle into the stitches as if you were getting ready to purl them).

2 Drop the cable needle and let it hang loosely at the back of the knitting.

3 Move the yarn to the back of the knitting needles but in front of the cable needle.

Working in front of the cable needle, knit the next 3 stitches on the left needle.

4 Slide the held stitches to the right side of the cable needle and knit them using the right needle. The cable is complete. Work the stitches after the cable according to the pattern.

5 When you work the wrong side, you don't need to do anything special with the cable stitches since they have already been crossed. The cable stitches will be a little crowded, but simply knit or purl them according to the pattern.

Practice Swatch: Cable

Learn how to knit cables by making a practice swatch using worsted weight yarn and US size 8 (5 mm) 9" (23 cm) single-pointed needles (see page 00 for more information about materials and needles).

Cast on 24 sts and work as follows:

Row 1: P4, k6, p4, k6, p4.

Row 2: K4, p6, k4, p6, k4

Row 3: P4, k6, p4, k6, p4.

Row 4: K4, p6, k4, p6, k4

Row 5: P4, 6-st RKC, p4, 6-st LKC, p4

Row 6: K4, p6, k4, p6, k4

Continue rows 1 to 6 until you are comfortable with making both right- and left-slanting cables. Work rows 1 and 2 again and then bind off.

INCREASING AND DECREASING STITCHES

The cables cause the knit fabric to contract from side to side. The garter stitch border before and after the cable section will not lie flat unless stitches are added and subtracted to compensate.

Knit Front and Back Increase (kf&b)

This is the most simple and easily learned increase. It is often referred to as the bar increase because a small bar is formed on the right side of the knitting.

1 First knit in the usual way but don't take the new stitch off your needle.

(continued)

Knit Front and Back Increase (kf&b) (continued)

2 Pivot the right needle to the back of the left needle and insert it knitwise (from front to back) into the back loop of the same stitch just worked.

3 Make another stitch into the back loop and pull the new loop through to the front of the knitting. Slip the old stitch off the left needle along with the 2 stitches just made on the right needle. There are now 2 stitches in place of one.

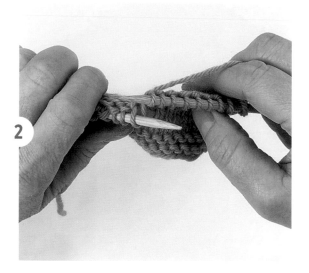

Knit Two Together Decrease (k2tog)

1 Insert the right needle knitwise into the next 2 stitches on the left needle.

2 Wrap the yarn around the right needle.

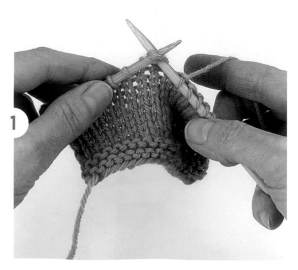

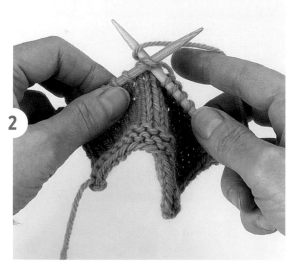

3 Knit these 2 stitches at the same time as if they were 1 stitch. There is now 1 stitch in the place of 2 stitches.

Practice Swatch: Increasing and Decreasing

Practice increasing and decreasing stitches by making a practice swatch using worsted weight yarn and US size 8 (5 mm) 9" (23 cm) single-pointed needles (see page 00 for more information about materials and needles).

Cast on 12 sts.

Row 1: Knit.

Row 2: Purl.

Row 3: K1, kf&b, knit until 2 sts remain, kf&b, k1, there will now be 14 sts.

Row 4: Purl.

Rows 5 to 10: Repeat rows 3 and 4 three more times, there will now be 20 sts.

Row 11: K1, k2tog, knit until 3 sts remain, k2tog, k1—18 sts remain.

Row 12: Purl.

Rows 13 to 18: Repeat rows 11 and 12 three more times—12 sts remain.

Bind off.

STEAM BLOCKING

If you don't have the time for damp blocking or if you are working on a smaller item, then steam blocking can be very effective. Keep in mind that this method uses hot steam and is not appropriate for any yarns that contain acrylic or nylon.

To steam block, hold the steam iron about 1" (2.5 cm) above the item and allow the steam to penetrate the fabric. In stages, set the iron aside and use your hand to smooth out the fabric and make sure the width is consistent. Also, pay careful attention to the edges, making sure they are straight and even. If the item you're blocking needs to be stretched or needs to conform to a particular shape, then use rustproof T-pins to pin into place on the ironing board. Leave the item on the board until it is completely dry.

HOW TO MODIFY THE PATTERN TO FIT YOUR PHONE

First you need to measure your phone. Measure the lengthwise circumference and add the length you want for a flap (the pattern allows for a total length of 14" [35.5 cm]). Measure the widthwise circumference and add ¼" (6 mm).

The pattern is set up with two cables. Beginning with step 3, there are 3 stitches to the outside edge of each cable and 3 stitches between the cables. Don't change the number of stitches in the cable but add or subtract stitches to the side and middle bands as necessary to obtain the proper width for your phone. Whatever number you determine, keep in mind that the cast-on row and step 1 use 2 fewer stitches. Likewise, 4 stitches are subtracted (2 from each cable) immediately before the bind-off row in step 4.

To change the length, add or subtract the number of 6-row cable repeats as necessary.

How to Knit the Phone Case

FINISHED DIMENSIONS

- 5½" (14 cm) by 3¼" (8 cm)

1 **Cast on**
19 stitches.

2 Knit flap edging and set-up rows for the cable section.

Row 1 (WS): Knit

Row 2: Knit

Row 3: K5, kf&b, k7, kf&b, k5. There should be 21 sts.

3 Establish cable pattern.

Row 1 (RS): K9, p3, k9.

Row 2: K3, p6, k3, p6, k3.

Row 3: K3, 6-st RKC, p3, 6-st LKC, k3.

Row 4: K3, p6, k3, p6, k3.

Row 5: K9, p3, k9.

Row 6: K3, p6, k3, p6, k3.

Repeat cable pattern (rows 1 through 6) 13 more times for a total of 15 cables. The length from the cast-on row should be approximately 12¾" (32 cm). It is important to end on row 6 of the cable pattern. If necessary, make your case a bit longer; the extra length will be used in the flap.

4 Finish last cable and knit top edging.

Row 1 (RS): K9, p3, k9.

Row 2: K3, p6, k3, p6, k3.

Row 3: K3, 6-st RKC, p3, 6-st LKC, k3.

Row 4: K3, p6, k3, p6, k3.

Row 5: K4, [k2tog] twice, k1, p3, k1, [k2tog] twice, k4—17 sts remain.

Rows 6 to 10: Knit

Bind off loosely and evenly.

5 Weave in loose ends. Steam block the strip on ironing board or blocking board: steam thoroughly and pin to a dimension of 3¼" (8 cm) wide by 14" (35.5 cm) long. Allow strip to rest until completely dry.

6 Lay the strip wrong side facing up on a table with the straight top edge at the bottom. Fold with the top edge up so that it forms a pocket deep enough to fully enclose the device. Pin the folded portion in place; the curved flap portion will remain free.

7 Cut a strand of the yarn about 24" (61 cm) long and thread on a yarn needle. Beginning at the fold, whip stitch the pocket edges closed. When starting, leave a tail at least 8" (20 cm) long that can be woven in when whip stitch is complete.

8 Work the whip stitch in the 'valley' between the garter ridges along the edge, going under just one strand on the front and then one strand on the back.

9 When the pocket edge has been whip stitched closed, cut the yarn leaving a tail at least 8" (20 cm) long. Weave in the ends to secure. Repeat for other side.

10 If desired, attach Velcro coins to wrong side of flap and right side of pocket for closure. Use thread to match yarn; white thread was used here for clarity.

6

8

7

10

Shaping

One of the reasons knitting is so versatile is that it's easy to shape an item by either increasing or decreasing the number of stitches. In this section you will learn different methods for increasing and decreasing, the effect and appearance of each method, and which methods to use for different situations.

Felted Christmas Tree

What could be a better way to learn about increases and decreases than making a felted fir tree? Perhaps you've felted wool accidently by putting a sweater in the washer. You know that the sweater shrank dramatically and assumed the texture of thick felt. You'll be felting this tree on purpose in your home washer once the basic knitting is completed. One of the advantages of felting for a new knitter is the fact that the individual stitches can no longer be seen once the process is completed. That means that irregularities and uneven stitches disappear! So, don't be a perfectionist, learn some new skills and have some fun. To decorate your tree for Christmas, you can add bobble ornaments and yarn garlands after the felting is completed. Pattern begins on page 86.

WHAT YOU'LL LEARN...

- How to increase the number of stitches using the following techniques:
  Knit front and back (kf&b)
  Purl front and back (pf&b)
  Using cable cast-on to add stitches at the beginning of a row
- How to decrease the number of stitches using: Knit two together (k2tog)

- How to make I-cord
- How to fell knitted wool
- How to make a crochet chain
- How to knit bobbles

WHAT YOU'LL NEED...

YARN

- For Christmas tree: medium weight 100% wool yarn or wool and mohair blend
  Green: 358 yd (327 m)
  Red: 18 yd (16.5 m)
  Brown: 8 yd (7.5 m)

  Shown: Brown Sheep Company *Lamb's Pride Worsted* (85% wool, 15% mohair; 190 yd [174 m] per 4 oz [113 g] skein); Deep Pine, color M-172; 2 skeins; Ruby Red, color M-180, 1 skein; Sable, color M-07, 1 skein

(DO NOT use any yarn that is labeled washable or super wash). The wool and mohair blend used for this project gives a fuzzy finish. If you prefer a smoother texture, then choose a 100% wool yarn without any mohair

(continued)

WHAT YOU'LL NEED...........................

YARN (continued)

- For bobble ornaments: lightweight metallic yarn in red and gold, 52 yd (48 m) per color

  Shown: Tahki Stacy Charles/Filatura di Crosa *New Smoking* (65% rayon, 35% polyester; 132 yd [120 m] per 0.88 oz [25 g] ball); gold, color 01; red, color 06; one ball each

- For tinsel: lightweight novelty eyelash yarn, 11 yd (10 m)

  Shown: Trendsetter Yarns *Aura* (100% nylon; 145 yd [133 m] per 1.75oz [50 g] ball); lime, color 9329; pearl, color 82; one ball each

NEEDLES AND NOTIONS

- US size 13 (9 mm) 24" (61 cm) circular needle or size required to achieve gauge

- US size 13 (9 mm) 7" (18 cm) double-pointed needles or same size as circular needle
- US size 7 (4.5 mm) 9" (23 cm) single-pointed needles
- Crochet hook US size K (6.5 mm) or size desired to make tinsel garland from novelty yarn.
- Yarn needle for weaving in ends
- Fray Check
- Green sewing thread
- Sewing needle
- Star decoration for tree top (purchased at craft store)

EQUIPMENT

- Automatic washing machine
- Wool wash soap or baby laundry detergent (low suds requiring little or no rinsing)

GAUGE

- Before felting: 11 sts = 4" (10 cm) in stockinette stitch
- After felting: 12 sts = 4" (10 cm) in stockinette stitch

Skills and Useful Information

INCREASES AND DECREASES

A very simple increase can be accomplished by knitting into the same stitch twice, thereby adding 1 stitch (knit front and back—kf&b). By knitting 2 stitches together at the same time (knit 2 together—k2tog) the number of stitches can be decreased by 1. There are actually many ways to increase and decrease in knitting, and each method results in a different look. The primary distinction is the direction in which the stitches slant—either to the right or to the left—after the increase or decrease. For example, the direction of the stitch slant is important if you are making the neck opening in a V-neck sweater. The stitches on the right side of the "V" should point to the right and the stitches on the left side of the "V" should point to the left.

Before starting the projects in this chapter there are some basic increases and decreases to be learned. Although knit front and back (kf&b) and knit two together (k2tog) were covered briefly in the Texture section, it's a good idea to review because these techniques will be used extensively in the two patterns that follow. Master all of the shaping techniques on the practice swatch before you jump into the projects. Please note **the increases and decreases for both projects are included in this section** so they can all be practiced on the same Swatch.

INCREASES
Knit Front and Back (kf&b)

This is the most simple and easily learned increase. It is often referred to as the bar increase because a small bar is formed on the right side of the knitting.

1 First knit in the usual way but don't take the new stitch off your needle.

2 Pivot the right needle to the back of the left needle and insert it knitwise (from front to back) into the back loop of the same stitch just worked.

3 Make another stitch into the back loop and pull the new loop through to the front of the knitting.

4 Slip the old stitch off the left needle along with the 2 stitches just made on the right needle. There are now 2 stitches in place of 1.

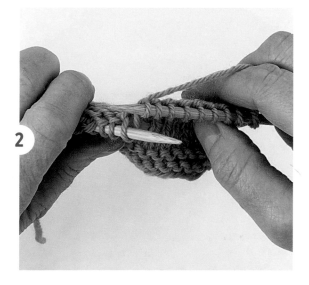

Purl Front and Back (pf&b)

1 First purl in the usual way but don't take the new stitch off the needle.

2 Keeping the working yarn in front, pivot the right needle to the back of the left needle.

3 Insert right needle purlwise (from back to front) into the back loop of the same stitch just worked.

4 Now make another purl stitch in the back loop.

5 Pull the new loop to the back of the knitting. Slip the old stitch off the left needle along with the 2 stitches just made on the right needle. There are now 2 stitches in place of 1.

Make One (M1)

The make one (M1) increases can slant to either the right or the left, but both increases have in common the fact that they make a stitch out of the horizontal bar or "ladder" that extends between every 2 stitches. The horizontal bar is picked up onto the left needle and then worked as a knit stitch. When working the new stitch the bar is given a twist to avoid a large hole in the knitting. The directional slant of the increase is caused by how the bar is picked up, either from the front or the back. This increase is sometimes referred to as a lifted increase.

Make One Right (M1R)—slants to the right

1 Working from back to front, insert left needle under the horizontal bar between the stitch on the right needle and the stitch on the left needle.

2 Insert right needle from the left (A) to the right (B) under the strand on the front of the left needle, thereby twisting it and preventing a hole.

3 Wrap the yarn around the right needle to form a new stitch and slip the new stitch and the picked-up strand off the left needle. One new stitch has been added.

Make One Left (M1L)—
slants to the left

1 Working from front to back, insert left needle under the horizontal bar between the stitch on the right needle and the stitch on the left needle.

2 Insert the right needle from the right to the left under the strand on the **back** of the left needle thereby twisting it and preventing a hole.

3 Wrap the yarn around the right needle to form a new stitch and slip the new stitch and the picked-up strand off the left needle. One new stitch has been added.

Yarnover (yo)

A yarnover is a very fast increase to work but keep in mind that it leaves a visible hole in your knitting.

1 Bring yarn forward between needles.

2 Lay the yarn over the right needle in a counterclockwise direction ending behind the needle. One new stitch has been added.

3 Knit the next stitch. Notice that the yarnover has made an extra loop on the right needle that is worked as a stitch on the next row. The yarnover loop can be worked as a knit stitch or purl stitch (shown).

Practice Swatch: Increasing

Practice increasing stitches by making a swatch using worsted weight yarn and US size 8 (5 mm) 9" (23 cm) single-pointed needles (see pages 6–9 for more information about materials and needles). As you practice the increases, notice how the stitches slant to the right or the left. Increases and decreases are rarely worked on the edge stitch; rather, one or more plain stitches is made first.

After each section of the swatch is completed feel free to repeat the section several more times for more practice. Notice that 2 plain stitches are worked at both the beginning and the end of the row and followed or preceded by the increase. The stitches in the middle are worked even (without increasing or decreasing) in either purl on the wrong side or knit on the right side.

Cast on 8 sts.

Knit Front and Back (kf&b)

Row 1 (WS): Purl.

Row 2 (RS): K2, kf&b, k2, kf&b, k2—10 sts.

Row 3: Purl.

Row 4: K2, kf&b, k4, kf&b, k2—12 sts.

Row 5: Purl.

Row 6: K2, kf&b, k6, kf&b, k2—14 sts.

Row 7: Purl.

Purl Front and Back (pf&b)

Row 8: Knit.

Row 9: P2, pf&b, p8, pf&b, p2—16 sts.

Row 10: Knit.

Row 11: P2, pf&b, p10, pf&b, p2—18 sts.

Row 12: Knit.

Row 13: P2, pf&b, p12, pf&b, p2—18 sts.

Row 14: Knit.

Yarnover (yo)

Row 15: Purl.

Row 16: K2, yo, k14, yo, k2—20 sts.

Row 17: Purl.

Row 18: K2, yo, k16, yo, k2—22 sts.

Row 19: Purl.

Row 20: K2, yo, k18, yo, k2—24 sts.

Row 21: Purl.

Make One Right (M1R) and Make One Left (M1L)

Row 22: K2, M1R, k20, M1L, k2—26 sts.

Row 23: Purl.

Row 24: K2, M1R, k22, M1L, k2—28 sts.

Row 29: Purl.

Row 30: K2, M1R, k24, M1L, k2—30 sts.

Row 31: Purl.

Continue practicing until you feel comfortable with the increases. When finished, don't bind off the swatch; save if for practicing the decreases. Take a moment to observe the different appearance of the increases.

DECREASES

All decreases are accomplished by working 2 stitches together at the same time. The slant is created by working either through the front of the loops or the back of the loops.

Knit Two Together (k2tog)—slants to the right

This is the easiest decrease to make and is easily remembered.

1 Insert the right needle knitwise into the next 2 stitches on the left needle.

2 Wrap the yarn around the right needle.

3 Knit these 2 stitches at the same time as if they were 1 stitch. There is now 1 stitch in the place of 2 stitches.

Purl Two Together (p2tog)—
slants to the right on the knit side

This is very similar to the k2tog but rarely used (you'll see it in the directions for the knit bobbles)

Insert the right needle purlwise into the next 2 stitches on the left needle. Wrap the yarn around the needle and purl these 2 stitches at the same time as if they were 1 stitch. There is now 1 stitch in the place of 2.

Slip, Slip, Knit (ssk)—slants to the left

1 This decrease is very similar to the k2tog except that the decrease is worked through the back loops of 2 stitches at a time. Working one at a time, slip the next 2 stitches knitwise to right needle.

2 Insert the tip of the left needle into the front loops of these 2 stitches.

3 Knit these stitches at the same time through the back loops as if they were 1 stitch.

Practice Swatch: Decreasing

Continue working on the practice swatch from increasing (page 79) to learn the decreases.

Row 32: K2, ssk, K22, k2tog, k2—28 sts remain.

Row 33: Purl.

Row 34: K2, ssk, K20, k2tog, k2—26 sts remain.

Row 35: Purl.

Row 36: K2, ssk, K18, k2tog, k2—24 sts remain.

Row 37: Purl.

Row 38: K2, ssk, K16, k2tog, k2—22 sts remain.

Row 39: Purl.

Row 40: K2, ssk, K14, k2tog, k2—20 sts remain.

Row 41: Purl.

Row 42: K2, ssk, K12, k2tog, k2—18 sts remain.

Bind off all stitches now or continue practicing as you desire. Take a moment to observe the different appearances of the decreases.

CABLE CAST-ON

As you learned in the Texture section, this method of casting on can be used in place of a standard long-tail cast-on, but it's also very useful for adding stitches at the beginning of an existing row or even in the middle of a row, for instance, when making a wide buttonhole. Insert the needle between the first and second stitch on the left needle and add as many stitches as required by the pattern following the step-by-step directions on page 47. When adding stitches at the beginning of a row it is not necessary to turn the needle in order to begin the next row of knitting.

FELTING IN A WASHING MACHINE

The felting process requires three elements: agitation, soap, and heat. Agitation comes from your washer set to the lowest water level. Also, put in some old jeans or tennis shoes or any other lint-free washable item to help bash your knitting around. A little bit of soap is essential. Use a special wool wash soap that doesn't need to be rinsed so you don't have to worry about too many suds (baby laundry detergent also works well). You need the hottest water your washer will provide. The best felting results will be obtained in a top-loading machine. If you have a front-loading machine it might take several cycles to obtain the desired amount of felting. If you want a smooth surface without too much fuzz, then put the item to be felted into a mesh laundry or lingerie bag before placing it in the washer.

Once you start the felting process, monitor the results every few minutes. If an item hasn't felted enough you can always put it back into your washer, but you can't reverse the process. If something becomes too small or heavily felted, you will be stuck with the result.

The hardest part of felting is putting your knit "baby" into the washer for the first time. Go ahead and throw it in. The stitches will begin to become less distinct, and eventually the surface will assume an all-over fuzzy or bumpy texture depending on how much you felt your item and the type of yarn you used. Stop the washer after just a few minutes and remove the item. Squeeze out the excess water and check the texture. If you can still see individual stitches, then return it to the washer for some more felting. Every time you pull an item out of the washer to check its progress, pull it from side to side as necessary to encourage it to assume its final shape, even if it's too big at this point. Sometimes the item you are felting appears to get bigger at first before the stitches begin to lose definition and the item begins to shrink.

Don't spin your item dry in the washer as this could cause permanent creases. Remove it and rinse in cool water in the sink. Wrap it in towels to remove excess moisture, pull it from side to side as necessary to establish correct shape, and then lay it flat to dry on a towel or a drying rack.

MAKING A CROCHET CHAIN

Practice the crochet chain using the same yarn specified for the practice swatches and a US size G (4 mm) crochet hook.

1 Make a slip knot (page 14) about 8" (20 cm) from the end of the yarn and place it on the crochet hook. Grasp the hook with your right hand. With your left hand, twine the working yarn over and under your fingers to create tension, and pinch the tail of the yarn (coming from the slip knot on the hook) between your thumb and middle finger.

2 Pass the hook under the tensioned strand coming from your left hand and rotate the hook a quarter turn to the left so you can grab a loop with the hook.

3 Pull the new loop through the existing loop on the hook. You now have a new loop on the hook. Continue in this manner, each time grabbing a loop from the yarn and pulling it through the loop on the hook. As you work, the chain will grow longer. Reposition your left hand as necessary, moving your fingers up the chain.

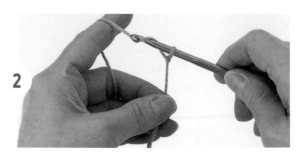

I-CORD

The modern version of this knit cord was named I-cord by Elizabeth Zimmerman. The "I" stood for "idiot" because Elizabeth felt any idiot ought to able to make it. After knitting a few rows you'll understand what she meant.

1 Using a double-pointed needle, start by casting on 4 stitches and knit 1 row (when casting on leave a tail at least 8" (20 cm) long). At the end of the row, instead of turning the needle to start a new row, push stitches from left side of needle to right side of needle. Start the new row, pulling the yarn across the back of stitches to work the first stitch.

2 Knit all 4 stitches. Continue in the same fashion, pushing the stitches back across the needle at the end of each row.

3 Within a few rows the knitting will begin to form into a tube. Work I-cord for approximately 6" (15 cm). Bind off stitches and cut yarn, leaving a tail at least 8" (20 cm) long.

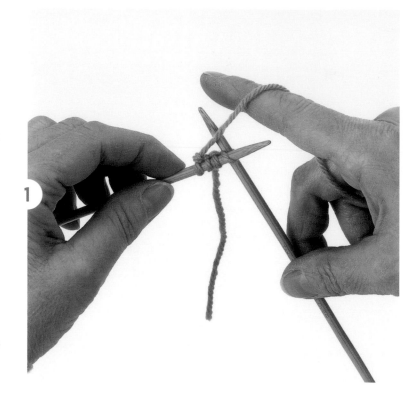

BOBBLES

Bobbles are little spheres that can either be knit into a pattern as a decoration or made separately with long ends that are used to attach them to an item. When knit separately the bobble can be used as a button or, as in the case of the Christmas tree, an ornament.

1A

1B

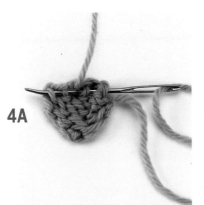

2

3

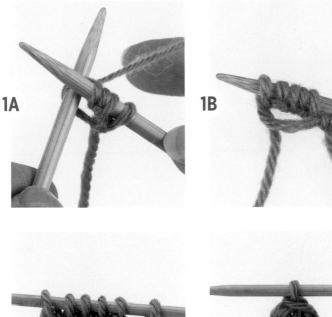

4A

4B

Cast on 2 stitches (be sure to leave a tail at least 8" (20 cm) long when casting on).

1 **Row 1:** K1, [k1, yo, k1, yo, k1] all into the next stitch—6 sts.

The picture on the left (A) shows row 1 after making the first 3 stitches into the second stitch on the needle (k, yo, k). The right picture (B) shows row 1 completed.

2 Using just the five stitches that have been made from one, work the following 4 rows:

Row 2: Purl 5 sts.

Row 3: Knit 5 sts.

Row 4: Purl 5 sts.

Row 5: Knit 5 sts.

3 **Row 6:** Now using all 6 stitches, [p2tog] three times.

Row 7: Slip 1, k2tog, pass the slip stitch over as if you were binding off. Cut yarn leaving tail at least 8" (20 cm).

4 Thread one strand of yarn from the tail on a yarn needle and work a running stitch around the open edge of the bobble (the purl side should be facing you) (A). Pull the running stitch tight and then tie both strands into a tight knot (B).

How to Knit the Felted Christmas Tree

FINISHED DIMENSIONS

- Before felting: 40" (102 cm) length (not including loop) and 24" (61 cm) width at widest portion Finished Dimensions

- After felting: 29" (74 cm) length (not including loop) and 20" (51 cm) width at widest portion of tree

It is very important that your stitches be somewhat loose before the item is felted. The stitches need to move and agitate against each other in order to felt. If your stitches aren't loose enough, then switch to a larger needle. As you can see from the photo above, the tree will shrink after felting, which is why two different gauges are shown.

CHRISTMAS TREE

The entire Christmas tree is worked with two strands of wool yarn held together (see page 36 for information about knitting with two strands of yarn at once). This pattern has a lot of rows, and as the tree gets taller the shaping order changes. You may find it helpful to use a pencil to make a tick mark next to each row as you complete it. At the end of the directions for each row in which the stitch count changes, you will find stated the number of stitches you should have after completing the row. It's a good idea to count your stitches and make sure your count is the same as the directions.

To help you keep track of your place you will often see the pattern specify whether you are on a right side (RS) row or a wrong side (WS) row.

In this pattern, the right side rows are knit and the wrong side rows are purled.

To accommodate the large number of stitches as the tree gets bigger, switch to using a circular needle (see page 48 for information about knitting back and forth on a flat item using circular needles).

In the skills section on pages 75 to 78 you learned about how to make increases and decreases that slant either right or left. Since the tree will be felted the individual stitches will not be visible so it isn't necessary to strictly adhere to the use of slanted shaping. Instead the simpler stitches are used.

Tree Top

1 Starting from just a few stitches, a triangular shape is formed by increasing at the beginning and end of every other row. After the triangle has reached the desired width it is decreased by binding off a partial number of stitches at the beginning of the last 2 rows.

Using larger needles and two strands of green wool yarn, **cast on** 2 sts.

Row 1 (WS): Purl.

Row 2 (RS): Kf&b, kf&b—4 sts.

Row 3: Purl.

Row 4: K1, kf&b, Kf&b, k1—6 sts.

Row 5: Purl.

Row 6: K1, kf&b, knit until 2 sts remain, kf&b, k1—8 sts.

Row 7: Purl.

Row 8: K1, kf&b, knit until 2 sts remain, kf&b, k1—10 sts.

Row 9: Purl.

Row 10: K1, kf&b, knit until 2 sts remain, kf&b, k1—12 sts.

Row 11: Purl.

Row 12: K1, kf&b, knit until 2 sts remain, kf&b, k1—14 sts.

Row 13: Purl.

Row 14: K1, kf&b, knit until 2 sts remain, kf&b, k1—16 sts.

Row 15: Purl.

Row 16: K1, kf&b, knit until 2 sts remain, kf&b, k1—18 sts.

Row 17: Purl.

Row 18: K1, kf&b, knit until 2 sts remain, kf&b, k1—20 sts.

Row 19: Purl.

Row 20: K1, kf&b, knit until 2 sts remain, kf&b, k1—22 sts.

Row 21: Purl.

Row 22: K1, kf&b, knit until 2 sts remain, kf&b, k1—24 sts.

Row 23: Purl.

Row 24: K1, kf&b, knit until 2 sts remain, kf&b, k1—26 sts.

Row 25: Purl.

Row 26: K1, kf&b, knit until 2 sts remain, kf&b, k1—28 sts.

Row 27: Purl.

Row 28: K1, kf&b, knit until 2 sts remain, kf&b, k1—30 sts.

Row 29: Purl.

Row 30: K1, kf&b, knit until 2 sts remain, kf&b, k1—32 sts.

2 After the triangle has reached the desired width it is decreased by binding off a partial number of stitches at the beginning of the next 2 rows:

Row 31 (WS): Bind off 6 sts, purl to end of row—26 sts remain.

Row 32 (RS): Bind off 6, sts, knit to end of row—20 sts remain. Tree top is complete

Tree Middle

3 The middle and bottom sections of the tree are work in the same manner as the top. To elongate the shape, more rows are worked between the increase rows. Be sure to keep track of your progress by making a mark next to every

2

row after it has been completed. Note that some of the increases are worked on purl (WS) rows using a purl front and back (pf&b) increase.

Row 33 (WS): Purl.

Row 34 (RS): K1, kf&b, knit until 2 sts remain, kf&b, k1—22 sts.

Row 35: Purl.

Row 36: K1, kf&b, knit until 2 sts remain, kf&b, k1—24 sts.

Row 37: Purl.

Row 38: Knit.

Row 39: P1, pf&b, purl until 2 sts remain, pf&b, p1—26 sts.

Row 40: Knit.

Row 41: P1, pf&b, purl until 2 sts remain, pf&b, p1—28 sts.

Row 42: Knit.

Row 43: Purl.

Row 44: K1, kf&b, knit until 2 sts remain, kf&b, k1—30 sts.

Row 45: Purl.

Row 46: K1, kf&b, knit until 2 sts remain, kf&b, k1—32 sts.

Row 47: Purl.

Row 48: Knit.

Row 49: P1, pf&b, purl until 2 sts remain, pf&b, p1—34 sts.

(continued)

How to Knit the Felted Christmas Tree (continued)

Row 50: Knit.

Row 51: P1, pf&b, purl until 2 sts remain, pf&b, p1— 36 sts.

Row 52: Knit.

Row 53: Purl.

Row 54: K1, kf&b, knit until 2 sts remain, kf&b, k1—38 sts.

Row 55: Purl.

Row 56: K1, kf&b, knit until 2 sts remain, kf&b, k1—40 sts.

Row 57: Purl.

Row 58: Knit.

Row 59: P1, pf&b, purl until 2 sts remain, pf&b, p1—42 sts.

Row 60: Knit.

Row 61: P1, pf&b, purl until 2 sts remain, pf&b, p1—44 sts.

Row 62: Knit.

Row 63: Purl.

Row 64: K1, kf&b, knit until 2 sts remain, kf&b, k1—46 sts.

Row 65: Purl.

Row 66: K1, kf&b, knit until 2 sts remain, kf&b, k1—48 sts.

Row 67: Bind off 8 sts, purl to end of row—40 sts remain.

Row 68: Bind off 8 sts, knit to end of row—32 sts remain. Tree middle is complete

Tree Bottom

Row 69 (WS): Purl.

Row 70 (RS): Knit.

Row 71: P1, pf&b, purl until 2 sts remain, pf&b, p1—34 sts.

Row 72: Knit.

Row 73: Purl.

Row 74: K1, kf&b, knit until 2 sts remain, kf&b, k1—36 sts.

Row 75: Purl.

Row 76: Knit.

Row 77: P1, pf&b, purl until 2 sts remain, pf&b, p1—38 sts.

Row 78: Knit.

Row 79: Purl.

Row 80: K1, kf&b, knit until 2 sts remain, kf&b, k1—40 sts.

Row 81: Purl.

Row 82: Knit.

Row 83: P1, pf&b, purl until 2 sts remain, pf&b, p1—42 sts.

Row 84: Knit.

Row 85: Purl.

Row 86: K1, kf&b, knit until 2 sts remain, kf&b, k1—44 sts.

Row 87: Purl.

Row 88: Knit.

Row 89: P1, pf&b, purl until 2 sts remain, pf&b, p1—46 sts.

Row 90: Knit.

Row 91: Purl.

Row 92: K1, kf&b, knit until 2 sts remain, kf&b, k1—48 sts.

Row 93: Purl.

Row 94: Knit.

Row 95: P1, pf&b, purl until 2 sts remain, pf&b, p1—50 sts.

Row 96: Knit.

Row 97: Purl.

Row 98: K1, kf&b, knit until 2 sts remain, kf&b, k1—52 sts.

Row 99: Purl.

Row 100: Knit.

Row 101: P1, pf&b, purl until 2 sts remain, pf&b, p1—54 sts.

Row 102: Knit.

Row 103: Purl.

Row 104: K1, kf&b, knit until 2 sts remain, kf&b, k1—56 sts.

Row 105: Purl.

Row 106: Knit.

Row 107: P1, pf&b, purl until 2 sts remain, pf&b, p1—58 sts.

Row 108: Knit.

Row 109: Purl.

Row 110: K1, kf&b, knit until 2 sts remain, kf&b, k1—60 sts.

Row 111: Purl.

Row 112: Knit.

Row 113: P1, pf&b, purl until 2 sts remain, pf&b, p1—62 sts.

Row 114: Knit.

Row 115: Bind off 26 sts, purl to end of row—36 sts remain.

4 In the middle of the final row of the tree you will change to the brown yarn for the trunk.

Row 116: Bind off 26 sts

Cut green wool yarn and change to brown wool yarn (double stranded) and knit to end of row working last 9 stitches in brown—10 sts remain.

For both colors, leave a tail at least 8" (20 cm) long to weave in later. The tree bottom is now complete.

Tree Trunk

5 The tree trunk doesn't have any increases or decreases. Continuing with two strands of brown wool yarn, work as follows:

Rows 117 to 136: Knit.

Tree trunk is now complete and brown yarn can be cut, leaving a tail at least 8" (20 cm) long to weave in later.

Tree Base

6 Now it's time to use the cable cast-on to add stitches at the beginning of the next two rows to form the top of the red base.

Change to red wool yarn, double stranded, leaving tails at least 8" (20 cm) long to weave in later. Work as follows:

Row 137 (WS): Purl 10 sts. At end of row turn work so right side is facing and add 8 sts using cable cast-on method; now there will be 18 sts.

After the cable cast-on is completed don't turn work, you are already oriented to begin row 138.

Row 138 (RS): Knit 18 sts. At end of row turn work so wrong side is facing and add 8 sts using cable cast-on method—26 sts. After the cable cast-on is completed don't turn work, you are already oriented to begin row 139.

Row 139: Purl.

Row 140: K1, k2tog, knit until 3 sts. remain, k2tog, k1—24 sts remain.

Row 141: Purl.

Row 142: K1, k2tog, knit until 3 sts. remain, k2tog, k1—22 sts remain.

Row 143: Purl.

Row 144: K1, k2tog, knit until 3 sts. remain, k2tog, k1—20 sts remain.

(continued)

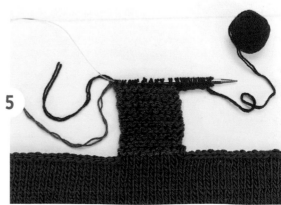

Row 145: Purl.

Row 146: K1, k2tog, knit until 3 sts. remain, k2tog, k1—18 sts remain.

Row 147: Purl.

Row 148: K1, k2tog, knit until 3 sts. remain, k2tog, k1—16 sts remain.

Bind-off all sts loosely and evenly. Weave in all ends.

Loop for Top (optional)

7 Using two double-pointed needles and two strands of green yarn cast on 3 stitches, leaving a tail at least 8" (20 cm) long. Make 6" (15 cm) of I-cord following guidelines above. Bind off stitches and cut yarn leaving a tail at least 8" (20 cm) long.

8 Fold I-cord in half and sew ends securely to the wrong side of the tree at the top to form a loop. Use the tails that were left from casting on and binding off. It is not necessary to be meticulous when attaching the loop, because individual stitches will disappear once the tree is felted. Weave in the loose ends.

Felting

9 Felt the tree in a washer according to the directions on page 82.

8

10

Bobble Ornaments

10 Using two strands of metallic yarn held together and the smaller single-point needles, make 15 red bobbles and 15 gold bobbles.

Tinsel Garland Trim

11 Making the tinsel garland trim will require a bit of trial and error on your part. The basic technique involves making a crochet chain using one or more strands of novelty yarn. The garland shown on the tree was made using a size K (6.5 mm) crochet hook and four strands of novelty yarn held together (two strands of ivory and two strands of green). If you've never made a crochet chain before, take a moment to practice using smooth yarn following the directions on page 83.

Once you are comfortable with making a crochet chain with smooth yarn, then begin making chains using the novelty yarn. The chain should be as long as desired plus about 1" (2.5 cm) to be folded to the back side for sewing. Make the desired number of chains for your tree tinsel. Each chain will be a different length depending on how close to the top you will be placing it.

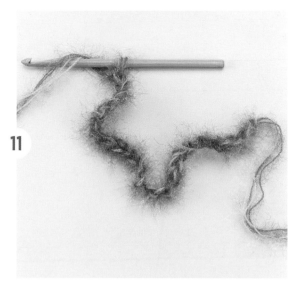

11

12

Finishing

12 First attach the tinsel to the tree using green sewing thread and a running stitch. The extra length should be wrapped around to the wrong side and secured with a few stitches. The ends from the crochet chain can be pulled through the felt and knotted or simply cut off.

13 Next attach the bobbles by threading two ends at a time on a yarn needle and passing the ends from the right side to the wrong side of the tree. Repeat with the remaining two ends and then knot all four ends tightly on the wrong side of the tree. Trim the ends to about 1" (2.5 cm) in length. If the bobble yarn is fraying then apply a drop of Fray Check to each end after it is cut.

14 The final touch is attaching a gold star to the top of the tree using sewing thread.

13

Leaf Edge Shawl

This lovely shawl has a treasure trove of increases and decreases. The basic triangular shape in the center is formed by increasing on each edge of the triangle on every other row. The leaf design is shaped using right and left slanting increases and decreases. The eyelet edging is created using a yarnover increase paired with a decrease. It sounds complicated here but once you follow the step-by-step directions you'll see how simple it really is to use increases and decreases to shape your knitting and add visual appeal.

WHAT YOU'LL LEARN..

- How to increase the number of stitches using the following techniques:
  Knit front and back (kf&b)
  Yarnover (yo)
  Make one left (M1R)
  Make one right (M1L)

- How to decrease the number of stitches using the following techniques:
  Knit two together (k2tog)
  Slip, slip, knit (ssk)

- How to knit and finish a triangular shaped shawl

WHAT YOU'LL NEED..

YARN

- Medium weight smooth yarn, approx. 625 yd (572 m). Since this is meant to be a cozy shawl, be sure the yarn is soft. Wool is a great choice for warmth, but if you can find a wool and silk blend or a wool and bamboo blend the shawl will have a better drape.

  Shown: Classic Elite Yarns *Wool Bam Boo* (50% wool, 50% bamboo viscose; 118 yd [108 m] per 1.75 oz [50 g] ball), 1632 Italian Plum; 6 balls.

NEEDLES AND NOTIONS

- US size 7 (4.5 mm) 29" (74 cm) circular needle or size needed to achieve gauge

- US size 9 (5.5 mm) straight or circular needle at least two sizes bigger than smaller needle for binding off only

- Yarn needle for weaving in ends

- Rust-proof pins for blocking

EQUIPMENT

- Iron

- Ironing board

GAUGE

- 18 sts = 4" (10 cm) in stockinette stitch

How to Knit the Shawl

FINISHED DIMENSIONS

- 53″ (135 cm)
  at widest point by 26″
  (66 cm) depth

1 To begin, you will cast on stitches and work a few increase rows to establish the basic triangle shape. Use the smaller sized circular needle. At the end of each row, you will find stated the number of stitches you should have after completing the row. It's a good idea to count your stitches and make sure your count is the same as the directions. See the note about working back and forth on a circular needle on page 48.

Cast on 3 sts.

Row 1: Kf&b, k1, kf&b—5 sts.

Row 2: Kf&b, k3, kf&b—7 sts.

Row 3: Kf&b, k1, p1, k1, p1, k1, kf&b—9 sts.

2 Make one increases (M1) are used on either side of the three center stitches to widen the leaves. It can be difficult on these beginning

rows to find the bar used to work the increase. Firmly stretch the stitches between the right and left needle to find the bar. Also, beginning on row 4, you will start the eyelet edging that is made with the first and last 3 stitches of the row.

Row 4: K1, yo, k2tog, M1R, k3, M1L, ssk, yo, k1—11 sts.

Row 5: K3, p2, k1, p2, k3.

Row 6: K1, yo, k2tog, k1, M1R, k3, M1L, k1, ssk, yo, k1—13 sts.

Row 7: K3, p3, k1, p3, k3.

Row 8: K1, yo, k2tog, k2, M1R, k3, M1L, k2, ssk, yo, k1—15 sts.

Row 9: K3, p4, k1, p4, k3.

3 Mark the right side (RS) of the shawl with an open stitch marker or a safety pin now (sufficient rows have been worked to allow the space). The right-side rows are even numbered, and they are also the rows in which all the increases and decreases are made.

Row 10 (RS): K1, yo, k2tog, k3, M1R, k3, M1L, k3, ssk, yo, k1—17 sts.

Row 11: K3, p5, k1, p5, k3.

Row 12: K1, yo, k2tog, k4, M1R, k3, M1L, k4, ssk, yo, k1—19 sts.

4 Stitch markers are added (pm—place marker) to delineate the center triangular section from this point forward. As your shawl progresses, more and more stitches will be added between the markers. When you reach a marker, slip it from the left needle to the right needle (sm—slip marker) and continue with the directions.

Row 13: K3, p6, pm, kf&b, pm, p6, k3—20 sts.

5 The increases for the leaf shape are complete and now decreases will be worked to taper the leaf to a single stitch. On right side rows (even numbered), a kf&b increase is worked to offset the decrease made to the leaf shape but the total number of stitches will not change on the

row. For this section, the stitch count will increase on wrong side (odd-numbered) rows. So, on both right-side and wrong-side rows, a stitch adjacent to each marker will be worked with a kf&b increase. After completing the first 23 rows, you can see that the shawl is beginning to form a triangular shape and the first set of leaf edging stitches are complete.

Row 14: K1, yo, k2tog, ssk, k4, sm, kf&b, kf&b, sm, k4, k2tog, ssk, yo, k1.

Row 15: K3, p5, sm, kf&b, knit until 1 st remains before marker, kf&b, sm, p5, k3—22 sts.

Row 16: K1, yo, k2tog, ssk, k3, sm, kf&b, knit until 1 st remains before marker, kf&b, sm, k3, k2tog, ssk, yo, k1.

Row 17: K3, p4, sm, kf&b, knit until 1 st remains before marker, kf&b, sm, p4, k3—24 sts.

Row 18: K1, yo, k2tog, ssk, k2, sm, kf&b, knit until 1 st remains before marker, kf&b, sm, k2, k2tog, ssk, yo, k1.

Row 19: K3, p3, sm, kf&b, knit until 1 st remains before marker, kf&b, sm, p3, k3—26 sts.

Row 20: K1, yo, k2tog, ssk, k1, sm, kf&b, knit until 1 st remains before marker, kf&b, sm, k1, k2tog, ssk, yo, k1.

Row 21: K3, p2, sm, kf&b, knit until 1 st remains before marker, kf&b, sm, p2, k3—28 sts.

Row 22: K1, yo, k2tog, ssk, sm, kf&b, knit until 1 st remains before marker, kf&b, sm, k2tog, ssk, yo, k1.

Row 23: K3, p1, sm, kf&b, knit until 1 st remains before marker, kf&b, sm, p1, k3—30 sts.

6 The next 20 rows will establish the basic directions that will be repeated over and over until the shawl reaches the desired width and is ready to be finished off on the top (or widest) edge. From this point forward, the stitch count will not be shown at the end of the row. Instead you will be given a reminder at the end of the rows in which the total stitch count increases. Just remember that the stitch count will increase by two on every right side (even-numbered) row as the leaf shape gets wider. As the leaf is being tapered down

to 1 stitch, the stitch count will increase on every wrong-side (odd-numbered) row. This is where the pin that you used to mark the right side rows will come in handy. Every 20-row repeat of the basic directions will increase the total stitch count by 20 stitches. The picture below shows the shawl after completion of row 43.

Row 24: K1, yo, k2tog, M1R, k1, sm, knit to next marker, sm, k1 M1L, ssk, yo, k1—2 sts increased.

Row 25: K3, p2, sm, knit to next marker, sm, p2, k3.

Row 26: K1, yo, k2tog, k1, M1R, k1, sm, knit to next marker, sm, k1, M1L, k1, ssk, yo, k1—2 sts increased.

Row 27: K3, p3, sm, knit to next marker, sm, p3, k3.

Row 28: K1, yo, k2tog, k2, M1R, k1, sm, knit to next marker, sm, k1, M1L, k2, ssk, yo, k1—2 sts increased.

Row 29: K3, p4, sm, knit to next marker, sm, p4, k3.

(continued)

5

6

How to Knit the Shawl (continued)

Row 30: K1, yo, k2tog, k3, M1R, k1, sm, knit to next marker, sm, k1, M1L, k3, ssk, yo, k1—2 sts increased.

Row 31: K3, p5, sm, knit to next marker, sm, p5, k3.

Row 32: K1, yo, k2tog, k4, M1R, k1, sm, knit to next marker, sm, k1, M1L, k4, ssk, yo, k1—2 sts increased.

Row 33: K3, p6, sm, knit to next marker, sm, p6, k3.

Row 34: K1, yo, k2tog, ssk, k4, sm, knit to next marker, sm, k4, k2tog, ssk, yo, k1.

Row 35: K3, p5, sm, kf&b, knit until 1 st remains before marker, kf&b, sm, p5, k3—2 sts increased.

Row 36: K1, yo, k2tog, ssk, k3, sm, kf&b, knit until 1 st remains before marker, kf&b, sm, k3, k2tog, ssk, yo, k1.

Row 37: K3, p4, sm, kf&b, knit until 1 st remains before marker, kf&b, sm, p4, k3—2 sts increased.

Row 38: K1, yo, k2tog, ssk, k2, sm, kf&b, knit until 1 st remains before marker, kf&b, sm, k2, k2tog, ssk, yo, k1.

Row 39: K3, p3, sm, kf&b, knit until 1 st remains before marker, kf&b, sm, p3, k3—2 sts increased.

Row 40: K1, yo, k2tog, ssk, k1, sm, kf&b, knit until 1 st remains before marker, kf&b, sm, k1, k2tog, ssk, yo, k1.

Row 41: K3, p2, sm, kf&b, knit until 1 st remains before marker, kf&b, sm, p2, k3—2 sts increased.

Row 42: K1, yo, k2tog, ssk, sm, kf&b, knit until 1 st remains before marker, kf&b, sm, k2tog, ssk, yo, k1.

Row 43: K3, p1, sm, kf&b, knit until 1 st remains before marker, kf&b, sm, p1, k3—2 sts increased.

7 Repeat rows 24 to 43 (a total of 20 rows) over and over until 11 leaf shapes have been completed (223 rows in total). You can make the shawl smaller

or bigger by changing the number of times rows 24 to 43 are repeated. For a smaller shawl, complete fewer repeats; for a larger shawl, add a few repeats more. If you follow the directions exactly, completing a total of 11 leaf shapes, then the total stitch count will be 230 stitches. Shown below is the shawl after the completion of the beginning 23 rows plus three repeats of the 20-row leaf sequence.

8 Once the desired number of rows have been completed for the body of the shawl, three additional rows are worked to finish the top edge. The edging rows should only be worked after the completion of a row 41; the wrong-side (odd-numbered) row that is made after the leaf shape has been tapered to 1 stitch. The stitch count will increase by one on the first edge row but after that will remain the same. It is very important that the top edge be bound off loosely; if it's too tight then the edge will curl. To bind off loosely, use a larger needle for just the right-hand needle when binding off. Since the right-hand

7

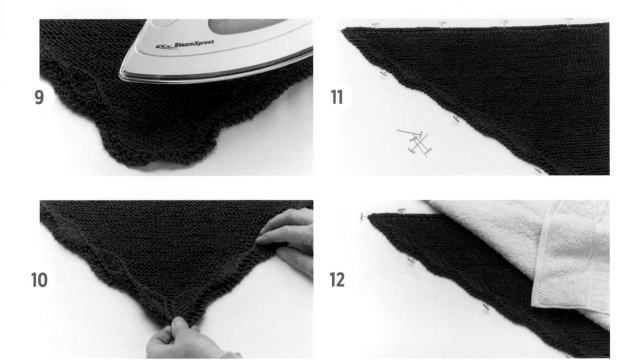

needle will only have 2 stitches at any time in does not need to be a circular needle; a straight needle works just as well.

Row 1 (RS): K1, *yo, k2tog*; repeat from * to * until 1 st remains, yo, k1—1 st increased.

Row 2: Purl all sts.

Row 3: Knit all sts.

Bind off all stitches loosely and evenly using a needle two sizes bigger than the needle used to knit the shawl.

Using the yarn needle, weave in all ends.

HOW TO FINISH THE SHAWL

9 After the knitting is finished, you will find that the leaf edging tends to curl under. This is remedied by steaming the edge using a steam iron. **At no point should the steam iron actually touch the knitting.** Hold the iron 1" (2.5cm) above. Lay the shawl on your ironing board and, working in sections, hold the iron above the shawl and allow the steam to penetrate the shawl.

10 Set the iron aside. Using your hands, gently stretch and smooth the leaf shape until it lies flat.

11 Once all the edges have been steamed, lay the shawl on a blocking board or carpeted floor and pin all three edges, placing a pin about every 5" (13 cm). The top edge should be pinned so that it is straight and even. The leaf edges are fluted so don't try to straighten the edge; rather, make sure the leaves lie flat and the triangle shape is consistent from side to side.

12 Cover the entire shawl with a towel that is just barely wet (wet the towel in the washer and then spin it dry). If necessary, use more than one towel. Leave the towel in place for at least four hours; it can actually be left on the shawl until it's completely dry. Once blocking is finished, your shawl is ready to wear.

HOW TO CARE FOR THE SHAWL

The center of the portion of the shawl is worked in garter stitch, which has a tendency to stretch. Your shawl should not be stored hanging. Instead, fold it and keep it on a shelf.

Knitting in the Round

One of the knitting world's most handy tools is the circular needle, which is two short needles that are connected with a cable. You've already learned how to use a circular needle to knit a project that has too many stitches to fit on a single-pointed needle. In this section, you'll learn how to use a circular needle to make a cylindrical item. In addition, you will find information for knitting with double-pointed needles to shape the crown of a hat and as a substitute for circular needles.

Felted Bag with Embellished Flap

A felted handbag is a great project for learning how to knit in the round. Part of the bag is worked in the round to form a cylinder followed by knitting back and forth on half of the stitches to make a flap. The bag is wet felted in your washer using agitation and hot water. This will transform the knit stitches into wool felt. When dry, the flap makes a perfect canvas for needle felting with wool roving. Look for roving assortments at your LYS. Bag instructions begin on page 105.

WHAT YOU'LL LEARN.....

- How to knit in the round
- How to combine knitting in the round with knitting back and forth
- How to pick up stitches and make I-cord handles
- How to seam the bag bottom using an overcast stitch
- How to embellish the flap with needle felting

WHAT YOU'LL NEED.....

YARN

- Medium weight, 100% wool yarn (DO NOT use any yarn that is labeled washable or super wash), approx. 200 yd (183 m)

  Shown: Cascade Yarns *220 Wool* (100% wool; 220 yd [201 m] per 3.5 oz [100 g] ball), 1 skein; as shown in model, color 4002; as shown in directions, color 8905

- Wool felt roving in various colors, approx. 0.25 oz (7 g) per color

  Shown: Frabjous Fibers *Three Feet of Sheep Spectrum Collection* (blue-faced Leicester top; 8 oz [229 g]); a scant amount of pink and green

NEEDLES AND NOTIONS

- US size 10½ (6.5 mm) 16" (41 cm) circular needle or size needed to achieve gauge before felting
- Optional: US size 10½ (6.5mm) 9" (23 cm) single-pointed needles can be used to knit the flap
- US size 10½ (6.5 mm) 7" (18 cm) double-pointed needles or size needed to achieve gauge before felting

- Yarn needle for weaving in ends
- Circular stitch marker
- Wool felting mat or foam pad (a dry sponge can also be used)
- Felting needle, 38 gauge or other all purpose size
- Scraps of variegated yarn (wool or wool blend to be used as border for flower petals)

EQUIPMENT

- Automatic washing machine
- Wool wash soap or baby laundry detergent (low suds requiring little or no rinsing)
- Zippered mesh laundry bag or pillow cover

GAUGE

- Before felting: 14 sts = 4" (10 cm) in stockinette stitch
- After felting: 17 sts = 4" (10 cm) in stockinette stitch

Skills and Useful Information

CIRCULAR NEEDLES

Circular needles come in a variety of lengths (measured from needle tip to needle tip). When used for knitting in the round, the length of the needle when joined from tip to tip will equal the circumference of the circle. Circular needles are used for knitting in the round (making a cylinder) as well as for knitting back and forth on a flat item with many stitches.

How to Knit in the Round on a Circular Needle

Using a circular needle to knit in the round is quite simple except that it is important that the stitches not be twisted when the circle is first made. Every pattern for knitting in the round will say something like "Join in the round being careful not to twist". You will learn in the practice swatch below how to join in the round without twisting the stitches.

Practice Swatch:
Knitting in the Round on a Circular Needle

Learn how to knit in the round by making a practice swatch using worsted weight yarn and US size 8 (5 mm) 16" (41 cm) circular needle (see pages 6–9 for more information about materials and needles).

1. **Cast on** 80 stitches. You will find information about casting on to a circular needle in the Texture section, pg 48.

   To avoid twisting the stitches, it is important that the chain of cast-on stitches does not spiral (or twist) around the needle. To avoid this problem, always make sure that the bumps at the bottom of the stitches are lined up facing the center of the circle formed by the needle. The stitches should be uniformly oriented as in the picture below, left.

   The stitches in the picture below right are spiraled or twisted around the needle. These stitches must be straightened before the knitting is joined in the round.

1

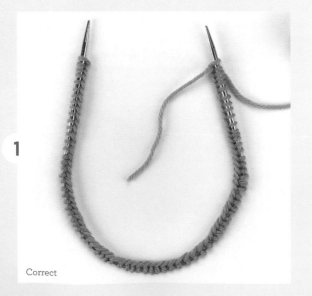

Correct

Incorrect

Length	Common Uses
16″ (41 cm)	Hats, small bags
24″ (61 cm)	Children's sweaters, tote bags
29″ (74 cm)	Children's and small adults' sweaters
32″ (81 cm))	Children's and small adults' sweaters
40″ (101.5 cm)	Medium and large adults' sweaters

The common needle lengths for knitting in the round are shown in the chart to the left. You can find shorter and longer lengths not listed on the chart, but most patterns use lengths shown.

A circular needle can be used to make an item that is slightly larger than its circumference, but it cannot be used to make an item that is smaller than its circumference. More stitches can be squeezed together but there's a limit to how far apart the stitches can be stretched.

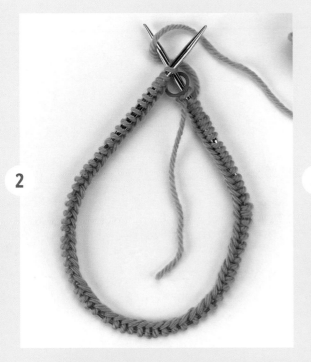

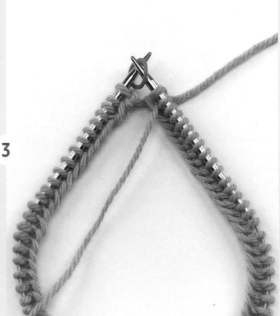

2. Line up the needles so that the last stitch that was cast on is on the right along with the working yarn. The first stitch that was cast on (the slip knot) should be on the left. Before making the first stitch, slip a circular stitch marker on the right needle. Insert the right needle into the first stitch on the left needle and use the working yarn to make a stitch. Pull the working yarn firmly on this first stitch to avoid

a gap where the knitting is joined together in the round.

3. Continue knitting around all the stitches on the circular needle until you reach the stitch marker. The marker indicates the beginning of the round (BOR) and it should be slipped to the right needle before each subsequent round. Every time you work around the stitches and back to the BOR marker, 1 round has been completed.

Stockinette Stitch in the Round Compared to Working Back and Forth on a Flat Item

Recall for a moment the beginning chapters of this book when you learned to make a flat item in stockinette stitch by alternating knit rows with purl rows. Think of what you learned this way: when knitting a flat item, the right side, the public side, is worked in knit stitch and the wrong side, the private side, is work in purl stitch. Because you are knitting back and forth, half of the rows are made using the knit stitch on the outside (the public side) and half of the rows are made using the purl stitch on the inside (the private side). However, when knitting in the round, for instance on a hat, you are always working on the outside (the public side). To make stockinette stitch in the round, **every** round is worked in knit stitch. You will see this clearly while making the bag when you stop knitting in the round about half way through and switch to knitting back in forth.

One interesting fact to note is that when knitting in the round, garter stitch is the opposite of stockinette stitch. Instead of knitting every row when working back and forth on a flat item, knit rows must be alternated with purl rows to execute garter stitch in the round.

NEEDLE FELTING

Needle felting is the process that binds wool and sometimes other fibers together to make felt. Instead of using water, felting needles with small barbs on the end are jabbed repeatedly through multiple layers of fibers. The jabbing (or stabbing) of the barbed felting needle locks the fibers together. The more times the needle is jabbed through the fibers, the tighter the fibers will lock together and the firmer the fabric will become.

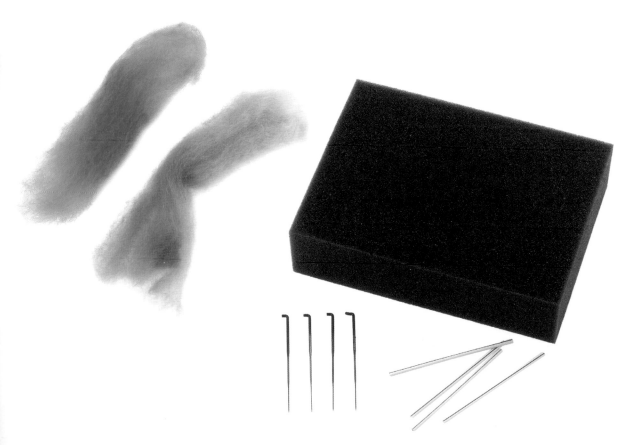

There are some very important guidelines to follow when you needle felt:

- The needles are very sharp! This is not a hobby for young children and the needles should be kept out of their reach at all times.
- Pay attention to the safety of your own fingers. Use a chop stick to keep the fibers in place instead of your fingers and keep your eyes on your work at all times.
- Protect your work surface. The needles will damage a hard work surface or be broken. The object being felted should be placed onto a needle felting mat, a piece of foam, or a dry sponge. The needle will stab through the felt and then slightly into the felting mat.
- The needles are breakable. Always move the needles straight up and down, not at an angle. When you finish using the needles, replace them in their covers. Don't stab the needle any deeper than necessary through the felt and into the protective felting mat.
- Lift your work up from time to time. The process of needle felting makes the fibers stick into the mat a bit so occasionally lift up your work and reposition it.
- Roving is simply unspun wool or other fibers. For use in needle felting roving is normally sold in short pieces of thick, ropey fluff that has been dyed. You can find both solid colored, commercially dyed roving and more artistic hand-dyed rovings with many colors or shades on the same piece. Just a few grams of roving, a quarter of an ounce or so, is a grapefruit size ball of fluff, which is more than enough of any one color for many projects. Look for color packs if you're just starting as this is an economical way to build a supply of colors.

How to Knit the Bag

FINISHED DIMENSIONS

- Before felting: 18" (46 cm) circumference by 12" (30 cm) depth
- After felting: 14" (35.5 cm) circumference by 8" (20 cm) depth

It is very important that your stitches be somewhat loose before the item is felted. The stitches need to move and agitate against each other in order to felt. If your stitches aren't loose enough, then switch to a larger needle. The photos above will give you an idea of the difference in the bag before and after felting.

Before felting

After felting

Begin at the Bag Bottom

Note: Charcoal grey provides a great contrast for the needle felted design but for clarity, blue yarn is used to show the steps in making the bag.

1 **Cast on** 60 stitches. Place BOR marker and join in the round, being careful not to twist (see page 102 for more information).

2 Work in stockinette stitch (knit all stitches) until the length from the cast-on row is 12" (30 cm).

Make Bag Flap

3 Bind off 30 stitches, leaving 30 stitches on the needle. Either knit back and forth on the circular needle (see page 48 for more information) or switch to single-pointed needles. Begin bag flap by knitting back and forth as follows:

Row 1: Knit.

Row 2: Purl.

Repeat rows 1 and 2 until the length of the flap (the portion that has been knit back and forth) is 11" (28 cm).

4 Bind off all stitches loosely and evenly.

I-cord Strap

5 (Note that the yarn in the photo used for picking up stitches and the I-cord is a

different color in order to show contrast. Your bag should be made using all the same color.) Four new stitches need to be added to the cast-off edge as the foundation for the straps. You will be working from the outside of the bag, using a separate ball of yarn (the leftover yarn from knitting the bag) and the double-pointed needles. Place the stitches as close to the corner formed by the cast-off edge and the bag flap as possible. Working from the right side, insert the needle from the front to the back going under two strands along the cast-off edge. Wrap the yarn around the needle as if you were knitting and pull a loop through and onto the needle. Continue in this manner until 4 stitches are on the needle. When starting the first stitch, be sure to leave a tail at least 8" (20 cm) long.

6 Using the stitches just added to the double-pointed needle, work I-cord for approximately 33" (84 cm). See directions for I-cord on page 84. Bind off stitches and cut yarn leaving a tail at least 8" (20 cm) long. Repeat for second strap.

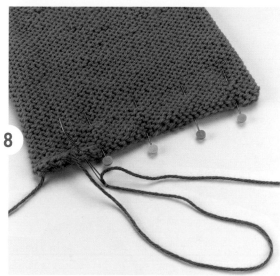

Seam the Bottom

7 Turn the bag inside out and pin the bottom opening closed with the right sides facing. The seam should be pinned parallel to the bound-off edge that was made before the flap was knit.

8 Cut a length of wool yarn (the same used to knit the bag) and thread it onto a yarn needle. (Note that the yarn in the photo used for seaming is a different color in order to show contrast. Your bag should be seamed using all the same color.) Start at the right edge, leaving a tail about 8" (20 cm) long. Insert the needle from the back to the front, going under the strands at the cast on edge (not through the individual yarn strands). Move about ½" (1.5 cm) to the left and repeat the stitch. Continue as established across the seam.

Make a few stitches very close together at the left edge and then weave in the yarn end to secure. Thread the other tail in the needle, make an extra stitch or two at the very edge, and weave in the ends to secure. Weave in all loose ends.

FELTING THE BAG

It is essential that the bag be put into a zippered mesh laundry bag or pillow cover before felting. If not, the straps can wrap around the washer post and be permanently damaged. Follow the general directions for felting on page 82. Be sure to check the bag frequently, pulling and tugging it into shape each time it is checked (this will encourage the final shape).

Once the bag is dried, the strap can be tied into a knot to make it the desired length. If desired, the strap can be trimmed to a shorter length. Once felted the knitting stitches won't unravel.

How to Needle Felt the Design on the Flap

1 After the bag is completely dry it is ready to be needle felted. Open the flap of the bag and place it on top of the needle felting mat or foam. You can work without a plan or draw a mock-up of your design before you start. Needle felting is a highly creative process with very fluid results, so allow your creativity to flow.

2 Begin by teasing apart bits of roving about as thick as a pencil. Lay the roving on the bag flap to outline the shapes of the flower petals, adjusting the colors and outlines until you are pleased with the general design. Use the felting needle to stab here and there and tack the design into place. Once you are happy with the general look, then stab the felting needle over and over into the roving until it is held firmly in place.

3 Now begin to fill in the petals with more roving, shading the colors if desired until you are pleased with the thickness. Just add a little bit at a time; you can always add more density but it's difficult to remove once it has been fully felted. Be sure to stab the surface of the petals completely and evenly to adhere all of the roving.

4 To make the center of the flower, pull off a pencil of a contrasting color of roving. Spit into the palm of your hands or sprinkle a few drops of water and then rub the roving quickly back and forth until it forms a dense, kinked cord. Coil the cord in the center of the flower, tacking it a bit at a time. Once in place, needle felt securely.

5 If desired, you can use bits of left over yarn from another project to outline the flower petals.

6 Using the same technique to make cords for the flower center, make flower stems and lay them in a curling fashion around the flower.

Needle felt securely into place and embellish the stems with some extra yarn if desired.

7 Flower buds can be made by rolling a small ball of roving back and forth in your hand (with a little bit of spit) to create a tight kernel of roving. Needle felt it into place but just around the edges so it adds some surface interest.

Once you are satisfied with your design, no further work is necessary. The needle felting process permanently attaches the fibers. Don't forget to pick up the bag and reposition it from time to time as you work. As you wear the bag, if some of the embellishment starts to come loose just take a moment to reattach it with your felting needle.

4

6

5

7

Easy Knit Hat

Making a simple hat is a terrific way to expand on the basic technique for knitting in the round. Once you get your stitches joined in the round you'll find this to be an easy, take-along project. Consider choosing an interesting yarn such as this self-striping yarn. Any small inconsistencies in your knitting will be disguised by the details in the yarn. The circumference of this hat is 20" (60 cm), which should fit most adults. Instructions begin on page 114.

WHAT YOU'LL LEARN

- How to knit a hat in the round using circular needles
- How to change to double-point needles from circular when decreasing
- How to add a decorative braid to the top of the hat

WHAT YOU'LL NEED

YARN

- Bulky weight, self striping yarn, approx. 105 yd (96 m)

  Shown: Viking of Norway *Balder* (100% wool; 137 yd [125 m] per 3.5 oz [100 g] skein); color 410, 1 skein

NEEDLES AND NOTIONS

- US size 11 (8 mm) 16" (40 cm) circular needle or size needed to achieve gauge
- US size 11 (8 mm) 7" (18 cm) double pointed needles or same size used to achieve gauge
- Circular stitch marker
- Yarn needle for weaving in ends

GAUGE

- 12 sts = 4" (10 cm) in stockinette stitch

Skills and Useful Information

USING DOUBLE-POINTED NEEDLES TO SHAPE THE CROWN OF A HAT

A knit hat is started on circular needles using the same guidelines as shown on page 102. The first section of knitting used to make a hat is simply a cylinder with a height of anywhere from 5" (13 cm) to 8" (20 cm) or more depending on the size of the hat. Once the cylinder is completed then the crown must be shaped, somewhat like the top of a dome.

The shaping is accomplished by dividing the stitches into wedges that are gradually decreased to form a tapered top. As the stitches are decreased to form the tapered shape, the circumference of the cylinder will become smaller and no longer fit around the circular needle. At that point the stitches must be transferred to double-pointed needles to finish the remainder of the crown. Before you transfer the stitches to the double-pointed needles you will already have established the wedges marked by a line of decreases (k2tog).

1 Continuing in the same stitch pattern, knit the stitches off the circular needle and onto four double-pointed needles. Transfer the stitches on one of the plain knit rounds in between the decrease rounds.

3

4

5

2 The most effective arrangement of the stitches is to put two wedges onto each needle. Divide the stitches evenly into quarters with one of the k2tog decreases at the end of each needle. It's best to place the beginning-of-round (BOR) marker in the middle of one of the needles, so start to transfer the stitches at the beginning of the last wedge before the BOR marker.

3 Once all the stitches have been transferred to the double-pointed needles, use the fifth needle for knitting the stitches one needle at a time. Knit all the stitches from the first needle onto the free needle. When that needle is empty it becomes the new free needle and is used to knit the stitches on the next needle and so on around the hat.

4 After working through the decreases you will reach the point where just 8 stitches are left, 2 on each needle. Cut the working yarn leaving a tail at least 8" (20 cm) long and thread it on a yarn needle. Working in same order as used with knitting, thread the tail through each of the stitch loops around the top of the hat.

5 Pass the needle through the hole on the top of the hat to the inside, and pull it firmly to close the hole in the top of the hat. Weave the ends into the stitches on the inside of the hat to secure the ends.

How to Knit the Hat

- Sized to fit a medium adult head
- 20" (51 cm) circumference by 8" (20 cm) height

1 **Cast on** 60 stitches and join in the round being careful not to twist. Place marker to indicate the beginning of the round. Knit 2 rounds, slipping the marker as you come to it.

2 To stop the brim from rolling a few rounds of ribbing are added.

Round 1: *K2, p2*; repeat from * to * to end of round.

Repeat round 1 three more times for a total of 4 ribbing rounds.

3 From this point on, knit all rounds. Continue knitting around and around until the length from the cast-on edge is approximately 5½" (13 cm). The rolled brim below the ribbing will need to be unrolled to obtain an accurate measurement.

4 Shape top. The stitches now need to be decreased to shape the crown. Work through all of the rows shown below. Change to double-pointed needles when the stitches will no longer fit comfortably around the circular needle. Use four double-pointed needles to hold the stitches and the fifth needle as the free needle for knitting. Arrange the stitches as shown in the Skills section (page 112) with 15 stitches on each needle to begin.

Round 2: *K13, k2tog*; repeat from * to * to end of round—56 sts remain.

Round 3: *K5, k2tog*; repeat from * to * to end of round—48 sts remain.

Round 4: Knit.

Round 5: *K4, k2tog*; repeat from * to * to end of round—40 sts remain.

Round 6: Knit.

Round 7: *K3, k2tog*; repeat from * to * to end of round—32 sts remain.

Round 8: Knit.

Round 9: *K2, k2tog*; repeat from * to * to end of round—24 sts remain.

Round 10: Knit.

Round 11: *K1, k2tog*; repeat from * to * to end of round—16 sts remain.

4

Round 13: Knit.

Round 14: *K2tog*; repeat from * to * to end of round—8 sts remain.

5 Finish the top. To finish the hat, cut the yarn, leaving a tail at least 8" (20 cm) long. Using a yarn needle, thread the tail through the remaining stitches and pass through the hole in the top of the hat to the inside. Pull the tail firmly to close the hole and weave the ends into the stitches in the inside of the hat to secure.

6

6 The last step is to add a decorative braid to the top. Begin by cutting three strands of yarn about 1 yd (0.9 m) long. Thread the strands on to the yarn needle and pass under a stitch on either side of the hole at the top of the hat. Pull the strands so that equal lengths are on either side of the center hole on top of the hat. There will now be six strands, three on either side of the hole.

7

7 Tie an overhand knot with all six of the strands. Divide the strands into two sections of three each and braid each section to the desired length. Tie an overhead knot at the end of the braid and trim the unused yarn.

8 Weave in all other ends and lightly steam block if desired.

Golf Club Covers

Making a set of golf club covers is a great way to reinforce your skills for knitting in the round. Instead of a circular needle this set is knit with double-pointed needles. Each cover has a different number of stripes that are made using different sections from a ball of self-striping yarn. Instructions begin on page 122.

WHAT YOU'LL LEARN...

- How to knit in the round using double-pointed needles

- How to make a pompom

WHAT YOU'LL NEED...

YARN

- Yarn A: medium weight, smooth yarn, approx. 240 yd (219 m)

  Shown: Plymouth *Encore* (75% acrylic, 25% wool; 200 yd (183 m) per 3.5 oz (100 g) skein); color 848, 2 skeins

- Yarn B: medium weight self striping yarn, approx. 92 yd (84 m)

  Shown: Jojoland *Rhythm* (100% wool; 110 yd (101 m) per 1.75 oz (50 g) ball); color 020, 1 ball

NEEDLES AND NOTIONS

- US size 7 (4.5 mm) 7" (18 cm) double-pointed needles or size needed to achieve gauge

- US size 5 (3.75 mm) 7" (18 cm) double-pointed needles or two sizes smaller that needle used to achieve gauge

- Circular stitch marker

- Yarn needle for weaving in ends

- Cardboard for making pompom form

- Scissors

GAUGE

- 16 sts = 4" (10 cm) in stockinette stitch

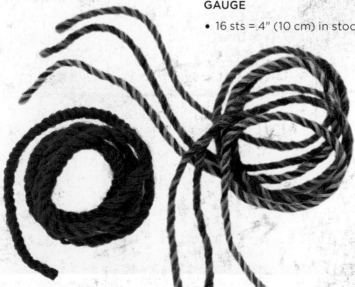

Skills and Useful Information
USING DOUBLE-POINTED NEEDLES
The circumference of the golf club cover is much smaller than the felted bag or hat. As was stated in the introduction to knitting in the round on pages 102 to 103 circular needles have a limitation. You can knit an item that has a larger circumference than a particular circular needle, but you cannot make an item with a circumference that is smaller than a particular circular needle. Double-pointed needles can be used to knit a circumference as small as a few stitches, and they are also used for shaping the crown of a hat. As a new knitter, avoid metal double-pointed needles; they are much too slippery. Use bamboo or wood instead. Also, don't use the very short double-pointed needles. Your needles should be at least 7" (18 cm).

Practice Swatch:
Knitting in the Round with Double-Pointed Needles

Learn how to use double-pointed needles to knit in the round by making a practice swatch using worsted weight yarn and a set of US size 8 (5 mm) 7" (18 cm) double-pointed needles. (see pages 6 to 9 for more information about materials and needles).

Double-pointed needles are sold in sets of four or five. The stitches are divided between three or four needles and the free needle is used to knit.

1. **Cast on** 24 stitches to one of the double-pointed needles. Your cast-on stitches, especially the slip knot, should not be too tight. Transfer the stitches to the other two needles so that there are 8 stitches on each needle.

2. Just as with knitting in the round on a circular needle, it is critically important to be certain the stitches are not twisted around the needles. Lay the needles down on a table in the shape of a triangle and make certain that the bumps at the bottom of the stitches line up facing the center of the triangle.

3. The triangle should be pointing up. The first stitch to be cast on (the slip knot) will be on the top left needle and the last stitch and the working yarn will be on the top right needle. For ease of understanding, the needles will be numbered 1 to 3. The top left needle is number 1, the bottom needle is number 2, and the top right needle is number 3. With the needles remaining on the table, insert the free needle into the first stitch on needle 1, the top left needle.

4. Use the working yarn coming from the last stitch cast on (needle 3) to make a loop around the free needle, then pull the loop through to make a new stitch. Pull the working yarn firmly on this first stitch to avoid a gap where the knitting is

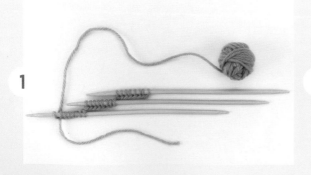

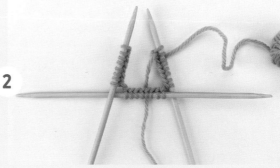

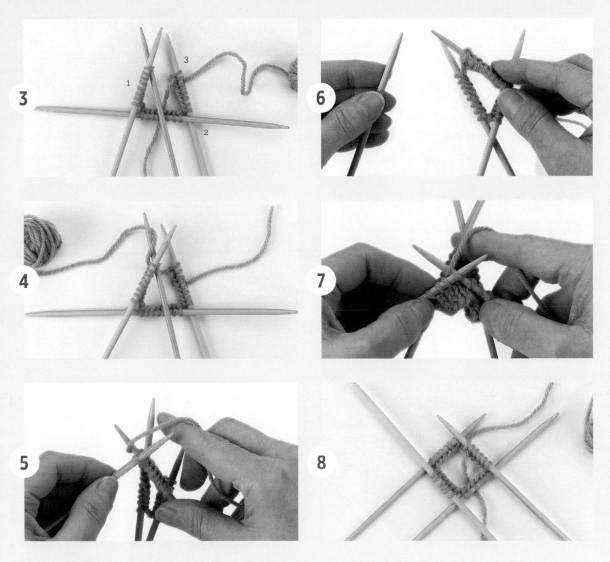

joined in the round. At this point, you can pick up the needles without fear of the stitches twisting.

5. Knit all the stitches from needle 1 onto the free needle.

6. When needle 1 is empty it becomes the new free needle and is used to knit the stitches on the next needle (needle 2) and so on.

7. The best way to deal with the extra needles holding stitches waiting to be worked is to ignore them! Focus on the two needles being used at any time and hold them at the front of your work, allowing the unused needles to fall out of the way to the sides and back.

8. It is also possible to divide the stitches onto four needles instead of three. If choosing this arrangement then the needles are arranged into a square instead of a triangle.

Use a locking stitch marker to indicate the beginning-of-round (BOR) stitch. Move the stitch marker up as you work.

MAKING A POMPOM

There are several different ways to make a pompom. You can purchase a pompom maker at your LYS or craft store or find lots of different directions online. Most of the methods you'll find involve sandwiching a center cord between a pompom form (circular or rectangular). Once the desired number of wraps have been made around the form, they are cut and then tied with the center cord. This method can be a challenge; the ends can get loose and it can be difficult to tie the center cord tightly enough. The method shown in the directions below might take a little longer but it provides better control.

There are a few things to remember about making pompoms. The width of the rectangle or form being wrapped defines how big the pompom will be. If you want a pompom with a 3" (7.5 cm) diameter then make a form that is a little wider than 3" (7.5 cm) and at least 6" (15 cm) long. The number of wraps will determine how thick or lush the pompom will be. If you want a floppy, more casual pompom, then don't make as many wraps. Also, the number of strands required is dependent on how thick the yarn is. The thicker the yarn the fewer number of wraps required.

1 Use a circular form such as a juice glass to draw a circle on cardboard and then cut it out with scissors. Measure the diameter and cut a piece of cardboard that is about ¼" (6 mm) wider that the circle's diameter and about 6" (15 cm) long. Cut a piece of yarn 30" (76 cm) long to be used as the pompom tie and set aside.

2 Wrap repeatedly around narrow width of the pompom form working from side to side as

you wrap so that the yarn does not bunch up too thickly in any one spot. Don't wrap the yarn too tightly; use a pencil or needle inserted under the wraps if necessary to make a bit of space.

3 Wrap the yarn around the form about 200 times. Remove the wraps from the form (take the spacer out first) and lay the bundle on top of the pompom tie. The wraps should be perpendicular to the tie.

4 Pick up the opposite ends of the center cord. Tie a single overhand knot and begin to draw bundle of yarn together. Adjust the center cord as necessary so that it is in the middle of the yarn pieces. When the pieces have been drawn together enough so they can be picked up, hold the bunch together with one hand and with the other hand

wrap one end of the center cord twice around the circumference of the sheaf. Tug firmly on the opposite ends of the center cord until it is drawn tightly around the sheaf and no more slack can be removed. Tie a double overhand knot to secure the pompom.

5 Insert scissors into the center of the loops on each side of the tie and cut the loops open. Be very careful not to cut the cord that was used to tie the pompom.

6 Keeping the center cords free (A), lay the cardboard circle over the pompom and trim the ends to a consistent length (B).

7 Fluff out the pompom by shaking vigorously. Continue trimming as needed.

5

6B

6A

7

How to Knit the Golf Club Covers

FINISHED DIMENSIONS

- 10" (25.5 cm) circumference by 12" (30.5 cm) length

PREPARING THE YARN

The self striping yarn (yarn B) that was used to make the contrasting stripes on the club covers varies in color from green to red. In order to be able to control the color of the stripe more exactly, wind the yarn into smaller balls so that each smaller ball starts with a different color.

MAKING THE CLUB COVER

1 Using smaller needle and yarn A, **cast on** 40 stitches and distribute the stitches on three needles with 14 stitches on needles 1 and 2 and 12 stitches on needle 3. Join in the round, being careful not to twist. Place marker to indicate the beginning of the round.

Round 1: Knit.

Round 2: *K2, p2*; repeat from * to * to end of round.

Repeat round 2, slipping BOR marker as you come to it until the length from the cast-on round is 6" (15 cm).

2 Change to larger needle and begin stripe pattern. Each club cover has a different number of stripes. If you are making the cover with three stripes, then follow all the rows of the pattern. For the one- and two-stripe versions, switch to stockinette stitch (knit every round) and yarn A after rounds 14 and 26, respectively. Shape all three covers the same, beginning with round 38.

Rounds 3 to 8: Knit to end of round. After completing round 6, cut yarn A, leaving a tail at least 8" (20 cm) long.

Round 9: Change to yarn B, *k5, p5*; repeat from * to * to end of round.

Rounds 10 to 13: *P5, k5*; repeat from * to * to end of round. After completing round 10, cut yarn B leaving a tail at least 8" (20 cm) long.

Round 14: Change to yarn A, *k5, p5*; repeat from * to * to end of round.

Rounds 15 to 19: Knit to end of round. After completing round 19, cut yarn A, leaving a tail at least 8" (20 cm) long. If you are making the club cover with one stripe, do not cut yarn A, and continue repeating round 15 until the length from the cast-on edge is approximately 10½" (27 cm).

Round 20: Change to yarn B, *p5, k5*; repeat from * to * to end of round.

Rounds 21 to 24: *K5, p5*; repeat from * to * to end of round. After completing round 22, cut yarn B, leaving a tail at least 8" (20 cm) long.

Round 25: Change to yarn A, *P5, k5*; repeat from * to * to end of round.

Rounds 26 to 30: Knit to end of round. After completing round 30, cut yarn A, leaving a tail at least 8" (20 cm) long. If you are making the club cover with two stripes, do not cut yarn A, and continue repeating round 26 until the length from the cast-on is approximately 10½" (27 cm).

Round 31: Change to yarn B, *k5, p5*; repeat from * to * to end of round.

Rounds 32 to 35: *P5, k5*; repeat from * to * to end of round. After completing round 33, cut yarn B, leaving a tail at least 8" (20 cm) long.

Round 36: Change to yarn A, *k5, p5*; repeat from * to * to end of round.

3 Shape top. All versions are worked the same from this point.

Round 37: Knit to end of round. To prepare for the decrease rounds, adjust the stitches while knitting this round so that there are 16 stitches on needles 1 and 2 and 8 stitches on needle 3. This will divide the stitches so that whole decrease segments are contained on the needles rather that split between needles.

Round 38: *K6, k2tog*; repeat from * to * to end of round—35 sts remain.

Round 39: *K5, k2tog*; repeat from * to * to end of round—30 sts remain.

Round 40: *K4, k2tog*; repeat from * to * to end of round—25 sts remain.

Round 41: *K3, k2tog*; repeat from * to * to end of round—20 sts remain.

Round 42: *K2, k2tog*; repeat from * to * to end of round—15 sts remain.

Round 43: *K1, k2tog*; repeat from * to * to end of round—10 sts remain.

Round 44: *K2tog*; repeat from * to * to end of round—5 sts remain.

4 Finish the top. To finish the club cover, cut the yarn leaving a tail at least 8" (20 cm) long. Using a yarn needle, thread the tail through the remaining stitches and pass through the hole in the top of the club cover to the inside. Pull the tail firmly to close the hole and weave the ends into the stitches in the inside of the club cover to secure. See the section about finishing the top of a hat for closing the hole in circular knitting on page 113. Weave in all loose ends.

MAKING AND ATTACHING THE POMPOMS

1 Cut out a cardboard circle with a diameter of 3" (7.5 cm) and a rectangle that is 3¼" (8 cm) by 6" (15 cm). Cut a strand of yarn A 30" (76 cm) long and set aside for pompom tie. Using one strand of yarn A and one strand of yarn B, wrap yarn around the narrow width of pompom form about 125 times. Finish the pompom as on page 121, steps 3 to 7.

2 To attach the pompom to the center top of the club cover, thread one strand of the center cord on a yarn needle. Pass the needle from the outside to the inside of the club cover. Repeat for the other strand working a stitch or two away.

3 Turn the club cover inside out and tie the two strands into a knot. To finish, weave in all loose ends.

Color

If you walk into any LYS or yarn aisle in a craft store, you'll be amazed by the combination of colors that line the walls and spill out of baskets. Once you're confident with your basic knitting skills, the urge to combine different colors of yarn becomes irresistible. This chapter will teach you four different ways to add color: stripes, color blending, slip stitch, and stranded knitting. Once learned, the basic concepts can add infinite variety to your knitting.

Striped Cotton Bathroom Rug

Hefty cotton/acrylic yarn worked in lively colors makes a very special striped bath mat. The easy-to-follow stripe pattern is a good introduction to the easiest way to add color to your knitting.

You can decide which side you prefer for the right side—the one with the corrugated line between the colors or the smooth line. Instructions begin on page 129.

WHAT YOU'LL LEARN...

- How to make stripes
- How to read a stripe sequence and apply it to a pattern
- How to make a striped bath mat

WHAT YOU'LL NEED...

YARN

- Bulky weight, smooth yarn
  Yarn A: Blue, approx. 185 yd (169 m)
  Yarn B: Yellow, approx. 155 yd (142 m)
  Yarn C: Grey, approx. 155 yd (142 m)
  Yarn D: Ivory, approx. 155 yd (142 m)

  Shown: Berroco *Weekend Chunky* (75% acrylic, 25% cotton; 119 yd [109 m] per 3.5 oz [100 g] ball)

  Yarn A: Cornflower, color 6905, 2 hanks
  Yarn B: Cornsilk, color 6910, 2 hanks
  Yarn C: Camp Stove, color 6958, 2 hanks
  Yarn D: Vanilla, color 6902, 2 hanks

NEEDLES AND NOTIONS

- US size 9 (5.5 mm) 24" (61 cm) circular needle or size needed to achieve gauge
- Yarn needle for weaving in ends
- Fray Check

GAUGE

- 14 sts = 4" (10 cm) in stockinette stitch

Skills and Useful Information

HOW TO MAKE STRIPES

Working in horizontal stripes is an easy way to introduce contrasting colors or textures to your knitting. You can change up the basic concept by making the stripes taller (with more rows) or shorter (with fewer rows). When knitting back and forth on a flat item, it is most convenient to make the stripes with an even number of rows. This can minimize the number of yarn tails that must be woven in and also maintain the consistent look of the stripes.

There's nothing complicated about the process of making stripes. At the end of a row with the first color, cut the yarn, leaving a tail at least 8" (20 cm) long. Start the next row with a new color, again leaving a tail at least 8" (20 cm) long. Tie the tails into a loose overhand knot to secure them (1). When the knitting is finished, untie the knot and weave in the ends.

The back side of the knitting on the row with the new color will have a corrugated line from where the two colors are intertwined (2). This side is generally considered to be the wrong side but you may find it more interesting and choose it as the right side.

When knitting back and forth, if the stripes are just a few rows wide or if the edge will become part of a seam, then the yarn can be carried along the side when it isn't being used instead of cutting it. Catch the unused yarn along the side of the work by looping the working yarn under it each time a new color is started (3). Stripes should generally be worked in even numbers so that the yarn is on the correct edge of the item when it's needed for a new stripe.

When knitting in the round it doesn't matter how many rounds compose a stripe. If you don't plan to cut the yarn between stripes, then it is important to change to a new color at the same location on the circumference.

HOW TO FOLLOW A STRIPE SEQUENCE

Quite often knit items will follow the same stripe sequence over and over until the work is completed. The pattern will specify the stripe sequence separately from the row-by-row directions. The row directions will give information about number of stitches, the pattern, the shaping, and so on but won't specify what color to use on each individual row. It's your job as a knitter to follow the stripe sequence at the same time as the row directions. If you find it hard to keep track of the stripe sequence, then jot the colors next to the rows or even write out the directions for each row along with the color that should be used. As you progress, check off the row.

Another helpful tool for keeping track of a stripe sequence is a row counter. Make a quick list of the row numbers and corresponding color it should be from the stripe sequence. At the end of every row, advance the row counter. If you lose your place, check the row counter against the stripe sequence list you made.

When you're new to making stripes, always mark the right side with a safety pin and move it along with your knitting. This will give you another visual clue as to whether or not it is time to change to a new color.

Because this is a book for a new knitter, the stripe sequence is presented two ways. It is stated in the introduction to the pattern and it is also stated explicitly in the row-by-row directions. See if you can figure out the next color from the stripe sequence in the introduction to the pattern instead of relying on the row directions.

How to Knit the Bath Mat

FINISHED DIMENSIONS

- 23" (58.5 cm) by 32" (81 cm)
- Stripe Sequence
  Yarn A: 8 rows
  Yarn B: 8 rows
  Yarn C: 8 rows
  Yarn D: 8 rows

1 **Cast on** 80 stitches using yarn A.

2 Follow the stripe sequence shown above while working all rows in knit stitch (garter stitch). To make the first repeat of the stripe sequence, work as follows:

Row 1 to 8: Using Yarn A, knit. At the end of row 8, cut the yarn leaving a tail at least 8" (20 cm) long.

Row 9 to 16: Using Yarn B, knit. At the end of row 16, cut the yarn leaving a tail at least 8" (20 cm) long.

Row 17 to 24: Using Yarn C, knit. At the end of row 24, cut the yarn leaving a tail at least 8" (20 cm) long.

Row 25 to 32: Using Yarn D, knit. At the end of row 32, cut the yarn leaving a tail at least 8" (20 cm) long.

3 Repeat the 32-row stripe sequence six more times for a total of seven repeats of the stripe sequence. At this point, the length from the cast-on edge should be approximately 31" (79 cm). If you want to make the rug shorter or longer, omit or add additional stripe sequences.

4 Finish the mat with one last stripe of yarn A as follows:

Rows 1 to 8: Using yarn A, knit.

Bind off stitches loosely and evenly. Cut yarn A leaving a tail at least 8" (20 cm) long.

5 Before weaving in the ends, decide which side will be used the most as the right side and weave the ends in on the opposite side. Weave in all ends, working parallel to the stripes so that either side can be used. Because the bath mat will get a lot of wear, apply a drop of Fray Check to the cut end of each tail after it has been woven in.

TIP Consider weaving in the ends as you knit, perhaps just before you put your knitting away each day; when making a project with many colors—and many tails—it can be intimidating to have to weave in all those ends at one time when you finish the project.

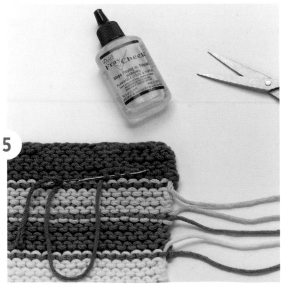

Slip Stitch Shawl

This gorgeous shawl is knit with a blended yarn made with wool, cotton, linen, and soy. The result is a lightweight but dense piece of fabric that becomes softer and a bit looser when wet blocked. Any lightweight or fine weight yarn in a solid color and smooth texture would be a good candidate for the pattern. Be sure to read the notes about blocking on page 133 if you substitute a delicate fiber such as cashmere or alpaca.

WHAT YOU'LL LEARN...

- How to wet block

- How to make a multicolor slip stitch pattern

- How to make a picot edging

- How to make a slip stitch shawl

WHAT YOU'LL NEED...

YARN

- Light weight, smooth yarn
Yarn A: Ivory, approx. 315 yd (288 m)
Yarn B: Grey, approx. 220 yd (201 m)
Yarn C: Seafoam green, approx. 220 yd (201 m)

  Shown: The Fibre Company *Savannah* (50% wool, 20% cotton, 15% linen, 15% soy; 160 yd [146 m] per 1.75 oz (50 g) skein)

  Yarn A: Natural 2 hanks
  Yarn B: Slate 2 hanks
  Yarn C: Seafoam 2 hanks

NEEDLES AND NOTIONS

- US size 7 (4.5 mm) 40" (102 cm) circular needle or size needed to achieve gauge*

- US size 8 (5 mm) 24" (61 cm) or long circular needle or one size larger than size required to achieve gauge.

- Yarn needle for weaving in ends.

  *The long needle length specified for the US 7 (4.5 mm) needle is necessary for the picot edging that is attached along the long side of the shawl after the main portion is completed. You may find it more comfortable to use a 24" (61 cm) circular US 7 (4.5 mm) needle for the body of the shawl (the slip stitch section).

EQUIPMENT

- Washing machine

- Towels

GAUGE

- 20 sts = 4" (10 cm) in stockinette stitch**

- 20 sts = 4" (10 cm) in slip stitch pattern before blocking

- 19 sts = 4" (10 cm) in slip stitch pattern after blocking

  **The gauge above for stockinette stitch is achieved using a fine/sport weight or light/DK weight yarn with a larger needle than is customary for that weight.

  For best results the gauge swatch should be worked in the slip stitch pattern (which is also a good way to become familiar with the stitch). The slip stitch pattern is a multiple of 4 stitches plus 3, so a good number to cast on would be 23 stitches. Follow rows 1 to 12 of the pattern in step 2 (page 134) to make a gauge swatch.

Skills and Useful Information

SLIP STITCH KNITTING

Slip stitch knitting is another easy technique for adding interesting color and texture to your knitting. Each color in the pattern is used by itself for 2 rows, even though it appears as if two colors were used on the same row. Working across the row, stitches are either knit or slipped from the left needle to the right needle (without being knit). The slipped stitch is not knit for 2 consecutive rows so that when the stitch is used again an elongated loop of the color from 2 rows before lies over the last color.

The most important element of slip stitch knitting is the technique used to slip the stitch. Slipping a stitch simply means it is transferred from the left needle to the right needle without working it (knitting or purling).

1 The stitch should be slipped as if to purl. To do so, insert the right needle into the stitch on the left needle as if preparing to make a purl stitch (the working yarn remains in back).

2 Pull the stitch off the left needle and onto the right needle. One stitch has been slipped.

Slip stitch patterns typically specify where the working yarn should be held when slipping the stitch. Usually, the working yarn is not seen on the right side when the stitch is slipped. So, the working yarn is held in back when slipping a stitch on a right-side row. Conversely, the working yarn is held in the front when slipping a stitch on a wrong-side row. The Slip Stitch Shawl is worked in garter stitch (knit every row), so you must pay attention to where the working yarn is.

With Yarn in Back (WYIB)

1 When slipping the stitch on the right-side rows, the yarn remains behind the work.

With Yarn in Front (WYIF)

2 When slipping the stitch on wrong-side rows, which are worked in knit, it is necessary to bring the yarn from the back of the knitting to slip the stitch.

3 After the stitch is slipped the yarn is returned to the front of the work to continue the pattern in knit stitch. Keeping the working yarn in front of the knitting, slip the stitch purlwise from the left needle to the right needle.

PICOT BIND-OFF

The picot bind-off is a technique that binds off the stitches and makes a decorative picot edge at the same time.

1 Cable cast-on 1 stitch. (See page 47)

2 Bind off 4 stitches (count one bind-off each time a stitch is lifted up and over another stitch and off the end of the right-hand needle).

3 Place the loop from the right needle back onto the left needle.

4 Repeat steps 1 through 3 across the row. Bind off the last stitch.

WET BLOCKING

Wetting a knit item can be a very effective means of blocking. Let the yarn label be your guide as to whether or not wet blocking is appropriate. **If the label says do not wash, then do not use wet blocking.** Also, if the garment is made from delicate animal fibers such as cashmere, angora, or alpaca, then pinning to dimension on a blocking board followed by a gentle spritz of water is more effective. If the item cannot be fully immersed in water as described below or if the piece is likely to be quite heavy (such as a bulky knit wool sweater), then

it can be pinned to the blocking surface first and moistened using a spray bottle filled with water.

Immerse the item in tepid water in your washer but **don't agitate!** Just get it wet. Spin most of the water out (don't spin it completely dry because this can leave creases). Alternatively, you can soak it in a sink or tub and squeeze out as much water as possible. Transfer the item to a large towel. It will be very heavy at this point and it's important that you pick it up in one compact bundle so it doesn't stretch. Carefully arrange the item on the towel

and roll it up to get as much moisture out as possible.

Never wring a knit item. Lay the piece out on a carpeted floor, mattress, or blocking board that has been covered with plastic (garbage bags work well). Covering the surface with plastic speeds up the drying process. Gently smooth the knit item into shape and use T-pins if desired to pin along the edges. Work from the center outward and frequently measure to maintain consistent widths and lengths or to ensure that the piece conforms to the pattern measurements and shape.

STITCH PATTERNS IN A MULTIPLE OF STITCHES

As your knitting skill increases you will most likely seek new stitch patterns or even purchase stitch guides to start making your own designs. Those patterns usually specify the number of stitches necessary to complete one pattern repeat or element. For instance, you might find a texture pattern that is 8 stitches wide. If that pattern is repeated over and over across the row, then a multiple of 8 stitches would be needed, and so the stitch guide would say the pattern is a "multiple of 8". In that case, the number of stitches in the row (excluding any border you might add) must be divisible by eight. In addition to the number of stitches for the pattern repeat (multiple of 8), there may be extra stitches needed just once to set up or finish the pattern. So, the stitch pattern will specify the multiple plus the one-time addition. For instance it might say, "multiple of 8 plus 2". In that case, the total number of stitches, **less two**, must be divisible by 8.

The slip stitch pattern used to make the shawl is a multiple of 4 plus 3. The pattern calls for 47 stitches to be cast on, which is eleven pattern repeats (4 × 11) plus 3 stitches. If you want to make the shawl wider or narrower, then add or subtract stitches in multiples of 4, for instance, a total of 51 or 43.

How to Make the Slip Stitch Shawl

FINISHED DIMENSIONS

- 9¼" (23.5 cm) by 64" (163 cm) before blocking
- 10¼" (26 cm) by 64" (163 cm) after blocking

1 It is essential that the cast-on row be worked loosely. Using the larger needle and the **cable cast-on** method, **cast on** 47 stitches using yarn A.

2 Change to the smaller needle and begin slip stitch pattern (A). Pay attention to the directions as to whether the stitch should be slipped with the yarn in front (wyif) or with the yarn in back (wyib). Also, do not cut the yarn when it isn't being used. When beginning each right-side (odd-numbered) row, bring the working yarn (the new color you are starting) up along the selvedge (side edge) from where it was used 4 rows below. When starting the first stitch with the new color don't pull the yarn too tightly; you want to make sure that the strand that is running along the selvedge remains loose and doesn't pull the side in (B).

2A

2B

Row 1 (right side): With color A, k1, *sl1 wyib, k3*; repeat from * to * until 2 sts remain, sl1 wyib, k1.

Row 2 (wrong side): With color A, k1, *sl1 wyif, k3*; repeat from * to * until 2 sts remain, sl1 wyif, k1.

Row 3: With color B, k3, * sl1 wyib, k3*; repeat from * to * to end of row.

Row 4: With color B, k3, *sl1 wyif, k3*; repeat from * to * to end of row.

Row 5: With color C, k1, *sl1 wyib, k3*; repeat from * to * until 2 sts remain, sl1 wyib, k1.

Row 6: With color C, k1, *sl1 wyif, k3*; repeat from * to * until 2 sts remain, sl1 wyif, k1.

Row 7: With color A, k3, * sl1 wyib, k3*; repeat from * to * to end of row.

Row 8: With color A, k3, *sl1 wyif, k3*; repeat from * to * to end of row.

Row 9: With color B, k1, *sl1 wyib, k3*; repeat from * to * until 2 sts remain, sl1 wyib, k1.

Row 10: With color B, k1, *sl1 wyif, k3*; repeat from * to * until 2 sts remain, sl1 wyif, k1.

Row 11: With color C, k3, * sl1 wyib, k3*; repeat from * to * to end of row.

Row 12: With color C, k3, *sl1 wyif, k3*; repeat from * to * to end of row.

3 Continue the 12-row slip stitch pattern until the shawl is approximately 63" (160 cm). In addition to reaching the approximate length, the slip stitch pattern must be worked through row 2 or row 8; in other words, you should have just finished 2 rows using yarn A.

4 Work an additional row and then bind off as follows:

Next row: With yarn A, knit

Continuing with yarn A, bind off all stitches loosely and evenly. When binding off, work all stitches in knit even though it is a wrong-side row. Cut yarn, leaving a tail at least 8" (20 cm) long.

5 Prepare to pick up stitches along long edge for picot trim. Mark the half-way point and the quarter-way points on the long edge of the shawl. You will pick up approximately 384 stitches, which is about 96 stitches per quarter of the length that is marked. It isn't critical to get exactly the same number; as long as you are within 5 stitches (plus or minus) of 384 you will be fine.

6 Using the longer US 7 (4.5 mm) needle, pick up approximately 7 stitches for every 12-row repeat of the pattern, for a total of approximately 384 stitches. Knit 1 row.

7 Work picot bind-off following directions given in the Skills section on page 133. You may have to adjust the number of bind-offs worked in the last set of steps depending on how many stitches you have left. When 1 stitch remains on the right needle, cut yarn, leaving a tail at least 8" (20 cm) long. Repeat for the other edge. Weave in all ends.

Block following the directions on page 133 for wet blocking.

Color Blend Scarf

There are many ways to bring drama to a knit item and color blending is one of the most interesting. Several different colors of the same yarn are used in the scarf but only two colors are used at any time (the two strands are held together). By changing the color combinations, one color undergoes a gradual metamorphosis into a new color. In addition to color blending, this scarf is knit on the bias, which emphasizes the drama of the colors and stripes.

WHAT YOU'LL LEARN. . . . .

- How to make color-blended stripes
- How to knit on the bias

WHAT YOU'LL NEED . . . .

YARN

- Hand painted yarns work beautifully for color blending. One variegated yarn was combined with two color-coordinated yarns with only slight color variations (semi-solid).

  Yarn A (variegated): super fine weight smooth yarn, approx. 235 yd (215 m)
  Yarn B (semi-solid): super fine weight smooth yarn, approx. 135 yd (123 m)
  Yarn C (semi-solid): super fine weight smooth yarn, approx. 100 yd (91 m)

  Shown: Claudia Hand Paints *Fingering Weight 100% Merino Wool* (100% merino wool; 175 yd [160 m] per 1.75 oz [50 g] skein)

  Yarn A: Passion Fruit, 2 hanks
  Yarn B: Mi Mi Melon, 1 hank
  Yarn C: Just Plum, 1 hank

NEEDLES AND NOTIONS

- US size 8 (5 mm) needle or size needed to achieve gauge
- Yarn needle for weaving in ends

GAUGE

- 19 sts = 4" (10 cm) in garter stitch (knit all rows)

Skills and Useful Information

COLOR BLENDING

The basic concept of color blending is to gradually change from one color to another using different combinations of yarn. A basic color blend uses three colors, A, B & C. Two strands of yarn are used at all times. Here is an example of how the colors can be used:

2 strands of color A
1 strand of color A and 1 strand of color B
2 strands of color B
1 strand of color B and 1 strand of color C
2 strands of color C
1 strand of color C and 1 strand of color A

Further variations can be achieved by changing the height of the stripe or the sequence of the color combinations.

Color blending requires switching different yarns in and out of the knitting. At the beginning of the color change rows, one strand of yarn will be discontinued and a new strand added. Cut the discontinued yarn, leaving a tail, and join in the new yarn. For both the old and the new yarn, be sure to leave tails at least 8" (20 cm) long to be woven in later.

BIAS KNITTING

Bias knitting creates rows that run at an angle to the straight edge of the item. The basic technique is very simple: 1 stitch is added at the beginning of the row and 1 stitch is decreased at the end of the row (for right side rows only). Because the rows run at an angle, there are more stitches in a row than would be used to create the same width in conventional knitting. The finished width can only measured after sufficient vertical length has been completed.

There are two options for starting a bias knit scarf. The total stitches for a row can be cast on and the bias knitting begun immediately (increase and decrease 1 stitch on every other row). This creates an angled point at both ends of the scarf (1).

If a straight end is preferred (2), then a beginning triangle is made by casting on 3 stitches and increasing at each end of the right side rows

until the desired width is reached. From that point, the basic bias technique is used until the scarf reaches the finished length, measured on its longest side. To finish the beginning triangle is worked in reverse by decreasing at each end of the right side rows until just 3 stitches remain which are then finished off.

How to Knit the Color Blend Scarf

- 59" (150 cm) by 3¼" (8 cm)

1 A beginning triangle is knit to make the squared-off end. If you prefer to make a scarf with an angled edge, then cast on 21 stitches and begin with row 18. As soon as possible, place a pin or locking stitch marker on the right side of the scarf (odd-numbered rows). As your work progresses, move the marker up so it can be easily seen if you need to remember whether you are on a right-side (odd-numbered) or wrong-side (even-numbered) row. All of the increasing and decreasing of stitches takes place on right side rows. The colors are switched in and out before beginning wrong-side rows.

Using 2 strands of yarn A, **cast on** 3 sts.

Row 1 (RS): Kf&b, k1, kf&b—5 sts

Row 2: Knit.

Row 3: Kf&b, k2, kf&b, k1—7 sts

Row 4: Knit.

Row 5: Kf&b, k4, kf&b, k1—9 sts

Row 6: Knit.

Row 7: Kf&b, k6, kf&b, k1—11 sts

Row 8: Knit.

Row 9: Kf&b, k8, kf&b, k1—13 sts.

Row 10: Knit.

Row 11: Kf&b, k10, kf&b, k1—15 sts.

Row 12: Knit.

Row 13: Kf&b, k12, kf&b, k1—17 sts.

Row 14: Knit.

Row 15: Kf&b, k14, kf&b, k1—19 sts.

Row 16: Knit.

Row 17: Kf&b, k16, kf&b, k1—21 sts.

(continued)

2 Begin bias knit pattern. The stitch count will remain consistent at 21 stitches until the desired length is completed. Don't be intimidated by the large number of rows in this pattern. The work goes very quickly, and switching the colors in and out will keep you engaged.

Change to one strand of yarn A and one strand of yarn B.

Row 18: Knit.

Row 19: Kf&b, k17, k2tog, k1.

Rows 20 to 33: Repeat rows 18 and 19 seven more times. (You will have worked a total of 16 rows since changing to yarn A and yarn B).

Change to two strands of color B.

Row 34: Knit.

Row 35: Kf&b, k17, k2tog, k1.

Rows 36 to 41: Repeat rows 34 and 35 three more times.

Change to one strand of yarn A and one strand of yarn B.

Row 42: Knit.

Row 43: Kf&b, k17, k2tog, k1.

Rows 44 to 57: Repeat rows 42 and 43 seven more times.

Change to two strands of color A.

Row 58: Knit.

Row 59: Kf&b, k17, k2tog, k1.

Rows 60 to 65: Repeat rows 58 and 59 three more times.

Change to one strand of color A and one strand of color C.

Row 66: Knit.

Row 67: Kf&b, k17, k2tog, k1.

Rows 68 to 81: Repeat rows 66 and 67 seven more times.

Change to two strands of color C.

Row 82: Knit.

Row 83: Kf&b, k17, k2tog, k1.

Rows 84 to 89: Repeat rows 82 and 83 three more times.

Change to one strand of color A and one strand of color C.

Row 90: Knit.

Row 91: Kf&b, k17, k2tog, k1.

Rows 92 to 105: Repeat rows 90 and 91 seven more times.

Change to two strands of color A.

Row 106: Knit.

Row 107: Kf&b, k17, k2tog, k1.

Rows 108 to 113: Repeat rows 106 and 107 three more times.

3 Continue with the color blend pattern that has been established by working two more full repeats plus a shorter section:

Rows 114 to 305: Repeat rows 18 to 113 two times.

Rows 306 to 345: Repeat rows 18 to 57.

4 Make a decreasing triangle to square off the end. If you prefer to make a scarf with an angled end, then bind off the stitches at this point and proceed to step 5, Finishing.

Change to two strands of color A.

Row 346: Knit.

Row 347: K1, ssk, k15, k2tog, k1—19 sts remain.

Row 348: Knit.

Row 349: K1, ssk, k13, k2tog, k1—17 sts remain.

Row 350: Knit.

Row 351: K1, ssk, k11, k2tog, k1—15 sts remain.

Row 352: Knit.

Row 353: K1, ssk, k9, k2tog, k1—13 sts remain.

Row 354: Knit.

Row 355: K1, ssk, k7, k2tog, k1—11 sts remain.

Row 356: Knit.

Row 357: K1, ssk, k5, k2tog, k1—9 sts remain.

Row 358: Knit.

Row 359: K1, ssk, k3, k2tog, k1—7 sts remain.

Row 360: Knit.

Row 361: K1, ssk, k1, k2tog, k1—5 sts remain.

Row 362: Knit.

Row 363: S1, k2tog, psso, cut yarn leaving a tail at least 8" (20 cm) long and pull it through last stitch to end.

5 Finishing. Weave in all ends. The scarf results in a lot of ends to weave in which can be a bit daunting. Allow yourself a few minutes to weave in ends every time you pick up the scarf to knit. It will be much easier to do this as you go along instead of leaving it all for the end. Steam-block lightly, if desired.

Color Block Hat

What an exciting project for learning how to knit with multiple colors! This pattern (page 147) is composed of three colors that are mixed in a lively play of stripes, blocks, and pin dots. The wide ribbing at the bottom can be worn folded up for a more tailored look or down for a hipster vibe. This hat never uses more than two colors at a time in any round. The pin dot, a single stitch in the middle of the block, is made using a knitting embellishment technique known as duplicate stitch.

WHAT YOU'LL LEARN..

- How to read a knitting chart
- How to read a pattern with multiple sizes
- How to knit with two colors at a time (stranded colorwork knitting)
- How to work duplicate stitch

WHAT YOU'LL NEED..

YARN

- Medium weight smooth yarn in three colors (the approximate yardage is shown in the chart above):
  Yarn A: brown
  Yarn B: green
  Yarn C: turquoise

  Shown: Malabrigo *Worsted* (100% merino wool; 215 yd [196.5 m] per 3.5 oz [100 g] skein)

  Yarn A: Pearl Ten , color 69, 1 hank
  Yarn B: Lettuce, color #37, 1 hank
  Yarn C: Bobby Blue, color 27, 1 hank

NEEDLES AND NOTIONS

- US size 7 (4.5 mm) 16″ (41 cm) circular needle or size needed to achieve gauge
- US size 5 (3.75 mm) 16″ (41 cm) circular needle or two sizes smaller than size used to achieve gauge
- US size 7 (4.5 mm) double-pointed needles or size needed to achieve gauge
- Circular stitch marker

- Yarn needle for weaving in ends and working duplicate stitch

GAUGE

- 18 sts = 4″ (10 cm) in stockinette stitch
- 19 sts = 4″ (10 cm) in stranded colorwork pattern

Skills and Useful Information

STRANDED KNITTING— HOW TO KNIT WITH TWO COLORS

The color blocks of this hat are made using a colorwork technique known as stranded knitting (sometimes referred to as Fair Isle knitting). The name derives from the fact that two different colors are used on the same row, with the unused color being carried along on the back side making floats, or strands. Stranded knitting is thicker than plain knitting because of the strands that are carried along the back side.

The challenge with stranded colorwork is what to do with the two strands; yarn A and yarn B. It's actually quite simple. The index fingers of each hand will do most of the work, keeping tension on their respective yarns, and your thumbs and other fingers will have the job of holding the needles. Twine yarn A around your left hand following the directions for Continental knitting on page 55. Twine yarn B around your right hand following the directions for English knitting on page 56.

1 To knit yarn A, insert the right needle into the stitch and, using your left finger to keep some tension on the yarn, move the needle up and over the yarn and then back towards you to make a loop and complete the stitch.

2 To knit yarn B, insert the right needle into the stitch and use your right finger to make a loop around the needle.

3 As you switch back and forth between the two colors, the unused yarn will make a horizontal line, or strand, across the back of the knitting.

Practice Swatch: Stranded Knitting

If you don't have any experience with stranded knitting, it's a good idea to practice with scrap yarn before diving into the hat. Cast on a multiple of five stitches and practice working the color chart. One of your hands is going to be inexperienced with holding yarn, but before long it will feel more natural. At the start of the round, look to see which color is going to be used the most and switch

that color to your dominant hand, which will do a better job of controlling the tension.

When you change from one color to another, stretch out the stitches on your right needle before you pull the new color across to begin knitting. This translates into a bit of slack in the new color and will help to maintain even, loose tension. The tension in stranded knitting has a tendency to be tight

because the strands on the back side are pulled too tightly, thereby making them too short.

	round number
	33
	32
	31
	30
	29
	28
	27
	26
	25
	24
	23
	22
	21
	20
	19
	18
	17
	16
	15
	14
	13
	12
	11
	10
	9
	8
	7
	6
	5
	4
	3
	2
	1

First stitch

■ Yarn A

■ Yarn B

■ Yarn C

HOW TO READ A COLOR CHART

To give you a sense of the anatomy of the hat, look at the photo below. The hat is knit in the round and the knitting begins with a wide band of ribbing. Next are several repeats of the stranded colorwork pattern with the colors switching between background, the squares, and the pin dots. The top is where the decreases to shape the crown are worked, along with a few more stripes.

The colorwork portion is made of segments of 5 stitches that are repeated over and over around the hat. A chart is used to represent the stitches in the colorwork section, but the directions are also written out for each stitch. Think of the chart as a road map. If you are driving somewhere, you can either look at the map or read the turn-by-turn directions. Many knitters find it easier to read the chart instead of the knitting directions, but if you're new to charts there are a few things to know.

The chart is a graphic format used to visually represent each stitch in the knitting, in this case the stranded colorwork section. Each square on the chart represents 1 stitch, and each line on the chart represents one round or row of knitting. Since the 5-stitch sequence is repeated over and over around the hat, only one repeat is shown. Start reading the chart from the bottom right corner; the first round of knitting is represented by the squares at the bottom of the chart. The brown squares represent yarn A, the green squares represent yarn B, and the turquoise squares represent yarn C. If you see a brown square (or two or three, etc.) then knit with yarn A. If you see a green square (or more), then knit with Yarn B instead. Read the bottom line from right to left. After you complete the first 5 stitches, then repeat line 1 from the chart (starting again at the right corner) over and over until you reach the BOR marker. When you finish knitting round 1 according to the chart, then start back at the right side and read line 2 from right to left (repeating over and over until the end of the round).

DUPLICATE STITCH

This is an embroidery technique that is used after a knit item has been completed. The embroidery stitch made covers the "V" of the knit stitch underneath. The yarn chosen for duplicate stitch should be the same weight or heavier than the yarn used to knit the item. The duplicate stitch used in this pattern is quite simple, just a row of single stitches spaced around the hat. However, duplicate stitch can be used for complicated motifs like snowflakes or names on a Christmas stocking.

1 Thread a yarn needle with the contrast color being used for the duplicate stitch. Starting on the inside or wrong side, insert the threaded needle from the wrong side to the right side at the base of the "V" formed by the knit stitch to be covered. On the first stitch only, leave a tail at least 8" (20 cm) long.

2 Insert the yarn needle under both strands of the "V" in the stitch above.

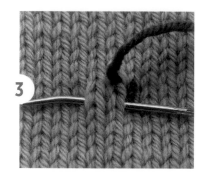

3 Insert the needle back into the base of the stitch, through to the wrong side, and back out at the base of the next knit stitch to be duplicate stitched.

4 Continue as before, inserting the needle under both strands of the "V" in the stitch above.

HOW TO READ A PATTERN WITH MULTIPLE SIZES

Oftentimes you will encounter a pattern that is written for multiple sizes, for instance, small, medium, and large. The directions for any given step might be very similar except the number of stitches or the length from the cast-on row varies by the size being made. A good example is the number

of stitches that must be cast on to begin a project; larger sizes will require more stitches than smaller sizes. Patterns often use parentheses to convey the number of stitches required to complete a similar step in different sizes. You will find a key next to the size chart that specifies how the parentheses will be used. In the pattern that follows, the directions are shown as Size 1 (Size 2, Size 3). The first step of the pattern says "cast on 80 (90, 100) stitches." If you're making size 1, then follow the direction before the parentheses and cast on 80 stitches. Size 2 is the first direction inside the parentheses; cast on 90 stitches. Size 3 is the second direction inside the parentheses; cast on 100 stitches. If no parentheses are used, then the direction is the same for all three sizes.

In certain parts of the pattern, the smaller size requires fewer rows to make a tapered shape. This is because the smaller number of stitches requires fewer decreases. In that case you will be instructed to skip the row and will see a direction that looks like this: "— (16, 17)." The dash signifies that the particular direction doesn't apply to the corresponding size.

TIP Once you've determined the size you plan to make, then go through the pattern and circle the direction that applies to your size with a pencil. Or photocopy the pattern and highlight the directions for your size.

How to Knit the Color Block Hat

The stockinette stitch gauge is shown in order to help determine the correct size needle. To be completely accurate, work a swatch in the color pattern. To do so, cast on a multiple of 5 stitches, join in the round, and follow the chart on page 145. A minimum of 70 stitches are required to fit around a 16" (41 cm) circular needle. If you prefer to make the swatch with fewer stitches, then used double-pointed needles (see page 118). It's important to swatch in the round since your gauge will be different compared to knitting back and forth on a flat item.

Size and Finished Dimensions

	Size 1	Size 2	Size 3
To Fit Size	5 to 10 year	Adult S/M	Adult M/L
Finished Hat Circumference	17" (43 cm)	19" (48 cm)	21" (53 cm)
Hat Height	9¾" (23 cm)	10" (25 cm)	10¾" (27 cm)
Approximate Yardage Required (total)	185 yd (169 m)	220 yd (201 m)	255 yd (233 m)
Yardage Yarn A	105 yd (96 m)	125 yd (114 m)	145 yd (133 m)
Yardage Yarn B	45 yd (41 m)	55 yd (50 m)	65 yd (59 m)
Yardage Yarn C	35 yd (32 m)	40 yd (37 m)	45 yd (41 m)

- Directions are shown in the pattern as follows: Size 1 (Size 2, Size 3)

1 Cast on stitches and make ribbing. Using smaller needle and yarn A, **cast on** 80 (90, 100) stitches and join in the round, being careful not to twist. Place marker to indicate the beginning of the round.

Round 1: *K2, p3*; repeat from * to *.

Repeat round 1 until length from cast-on row is 2" (2.5", 3") [5 cm (6.5 cm, 7.5 cm)].

2 Change to larger needle and begin stranded colorwork section. Don't cut the unused yarns. Instead, while working a plain knit round (without colorwork), pass the working yarn under the unused yarns before making the last stitch. This will create a loop around the unused yarns and bring them along as the knitting progresses. When starting a new color, be certain to leave some slack in the strand coming from the row where the color was last used (arrow).

3 Remember, the pin dot in the middle of the contrast blocks that you can see in the photo will be added after the knitting is finished. You can choose to follow the chart on page 145 or use the written directions that begin on the next page.

(continued)

3

The photo above shows the hat after completion of round 8.

Round 1: With yarn B, knit.

Rounds 2 and 3: With yarn C, knit.

Rounds 4 to 6: *With yarn C, k2; with yarn A, k3*; repeat from * to * to end of round.

Rounds 7 and 8: With yarn C, knit.

Round 9: With yarn A, knit.

Rounds 10 and 11: With yarn B, knit.

Rounds 12 to 14: *With yarn B, k2; with yarn C, k3*; repeat from * to * to end of round.

Rounds 15 and 16: With yarn B, knit.

Round 17: With yarn C, knit.

Rounds 18 and 19: With yarn A, knit.

Rounds 20 to 22: *With yarn A, k2; with yarn B, k3*; repeat from * to * to end of round.

Rounds 23 and 24: With yarn A, knit.

Rounds 25 to 33: Repeat rounds 1 to 9.

4 Shape the top of the hat. At this point you will begin the decreases to shape the crown of the

hat. The larger the size, the more stitches in the hat. So, the larger sizes will require more rounds to decrease their greater number of stitches. If you are making one of the smaller sizes, then skip the rounds that don't apply to your hat. Change to double-pointed needles when the stitches will no longer fit comfortably around the circular needle (see pages 112 and 113).

The color changes are not be included in the round directions below since they will vary depending on the size you are making. Work the color changes as follows: 7 rows with color B, 1 row with color C, and the remaining rows with color A (depending on the size you are making, color A will have fewer or more rows). After completing the rounds with colors B and C, cut the yarn, leaving a tail at least 8" (20 cm) long.

Round 1 for size 3 only: *K23, k2tog*; repeat from * to * to end of round—96 sts remain. Skip this round for other sizes.

Round 2 for size 3 only: *K10, k2tog*; repeat from * to * to end of round—88 sts remain. Skip this round for other sizes.

Round 3 for size 3 only: Knit. Skip this round for size 1, see alternative round for size 2.

Round 3 for size 2 only: [K43, k2tog] twice, 88 sts remain. Skip this round for size 1, see alternative round for size 3.

Round 4 for sizes 2 and 3 only: *K9, k2tog*; repeat from * to * to end of round—80 sts remain. Skip this round for size 1.

Round 5 for sizes 2 and 3 only: Knit. Skip this round for size 1.

From this point, all three sizes are worked identically.

Round 6: *K8, k2tog*; repeat from * to * to end of round—72 sts remain.

Round 7: Knit.

Round 8: *K7, k2tog*; repeat from * to * to end of round—64 sts remain.

Round 9: Knit..

Round 10: *K6, k2tog*; repeat from * to * to end of round—56 sts remain.

Round 11: Knit.

Round 12: *K5, k2tog*; repeat from * to * to end of round—48 sts remain.

Round 13: Knit.

Round 14: *K4, k2tog*; repeat from * to * to end of round—40 sts remain.

Round 15: Knit.

Round 16: *K3, k2tog*; repeat from * to * to end of round—32 sts remain.

Round 17: Knit.

Round 18: *K2, k2tog*; repeat from * to * to end of round—24 sts remain.

Round 19: Knit.

Round 20: *K1, k2tog*; repeat from * to * to end of round—16 sts remain.

Round 21: Knit.

Round 22: *K2tog*; repeat from * to * to end of round—8 sts remain.

5 To finish the hat, cut the yarn, leaving a tail at least 8" (20 cm) long. Using a yarn needle, thread the tail through the remaining stitches and pass through the hole in the top of the hat to the inside. Pull the tail firmly to close the hole and weave the ends into the stitches on the inside to secure. Weave in all other ends.

DUPLICATE STITCH

6 Duplicate stitch the pin dot in the center of the color blocks. The pin dot in the center of the color block is made by duplicate stitching the center stitch in the block. The color of the dot will vary depending on the background color of the block. The brown blocks (yarn A) will have a green dot (yarn B), the turquoise blocks (yarn C) will have a brown dot (yarn A), and the green blocks (yarn B) will have a turquoise dot (yarn C).

Begin with the bottom color section. Cut a piece of yarn B approximately 40" (102 cm) long and thread it on to a yarn needle. Duplicate stitch each of the blocks on the bottom color section. The yarn will float on the wrong side of the knitting from block to block. Do not pull the yarn tightly from block to block; the tension should remain loose. Leave tails at least 8" (20 cm) long when beginning and ending the duplicate stitch and weave in to secure ends when finished. The photo below shows the duplicate stitch being worked on the top row of blocks.

7 Repeat the duplicate stitch on the other colorwork sections following the color guide shown above.

8 To finish the hat, weave in all other ends. Steam lightly to block.

6

Lace

Knit lace has an airy, open appearance that beginning knitters often find intimidating. There's really nothing complicated about making lace. Eyelet holes created using a yarnover increase (yo) are paired with decreases in a set pattern. The combination of eyelets and decreases can be used to easily create scalloped edges and designs that flow almost as if they are sculpted.

Lace Scarf with Beaded Edge

A very easy lace pattern is used to create this stunning scarf made from hand-dyed sock weight yarn. The bottom edges are accented with a subtle row of beads that are added while casting on. Two identical halves are made and joined in the middle of the scarf so that both ends are accented with scallops. Scarf instructions begin on page 158.

WHAT YOU'LL LEARN...

- How to make a beaded cast-on edge
- How to make a simple lace pattern
- How to make a double decrease (psso)

- How to join two scarf halves with three-needle bind-off
- How to block lace

WHAT YOU'LL NEED...

YARN

- Super fine weight, smooth yarn, approx. 300 yd (274 m).

  Shown: Pagewood Farm *Alyeska* (80% merino, 10% cashmere, 10% nylon; 360 yd (329 m) per 4 oz (113 g) skein); color Peaceful, 1 skein

  Either wind the yarn into two balls of equal weight or weigh the total yarn before beginning knitting so you will know when approximately half the yarn is used and the second half of the scarf should be started.

NEEDLES AND NOTIONS

- US size 5 (3.75 mm) needles or size needed to achieve gauge, 2 sets
- US size 6 (4 mm) needle or one size larger that size needed to achieve gauge for three-needle bind-off
- Beading needle, big eye style, at least 2" (5 cm) long
- Seed beads, size 6 (3.3 mm); at least 62 beads in colors to coordinate with yarn
- Circular stitch markers
- Yarn needle for weaving in ends
- Rustproof pins for blocking

EQUIPMENT

- Iron
- Ironing board
- Blocking board or carpeted floor
- Towel

GAUGE

- 20 sts = 4" (10 cm) in stockinette stitch
- 23 sts = 4" (10 cm) in lace pattern

Skills and Useful Information

Most of the techniques used to make lace were presented in the shaping chapter; refer to pages 75 to 78 if you need to refresh your memory about increases and decreases.

PASS SLIPPED STITCH OVER (PSSO)

This is a technique that is used in combination with a k2tog decrease to create a double (2-stitch) decrease.

1 Slip 1 stitch from the left needle to the right needle. To do so, insert the right needle into the first stitch on the left needle as if getting ready to knit and slip it off the left needle an on to the right needle.

2 Knit the next 2 stitches together (k2tog) as if they were one.

3 Use the left needle to pass the slipped stitch over the decreased stitch and off the end of the needle. Two stitches have been decreased. Note: if a simple knit stitch (instead of k2tog) is combined with a psso, then only one stitch is decreased.

BLOCKING LACE

Lace must be blocked in some manner once finished or else it will have a bumpy surface texture and uneven edges. Start by blocking lace using steam, as described below. In most cases the lace will require additional blocking. Pin the lace to a blocking board, carpeted surface, or bed mattress and cover it with a damp towel or enclose it in a sandwich of two damp towels.

BLOCKING LACE

If the lace item you are blocking is small enough, you can start the process with steam blocking. A steam iron or steamer is used to penetrate your knit piece with steam that relaxes the fibers and evens out the stitches. At no point should the steam iron actually touch the knitting—it should be held an inch (2.5 cm) above.

1 Spread the item to be blocked on your ironing board or another heat-resistant flat surface and, working in sections, hold the iron above the item, allowing the steam to penetrate the work. Set the iron aside and use your hands to gently stretch and smooth the lace until it lies flat. Also, smooth and stretch any straight edges and coax the scallops into gentle points. Note: if you have any doubts about using steam, then skip this step.

2 Once the item has been steamed, lay it on a blocking board, carpeted floor, or bed mattress and smooth the item into shape. Use rustproof T-pins to pin the item to the blocking surface, beginning with the corners. Use a tape measure to make sure the width and length are consistent. Continue by pinning all the edges at frequent intervals. Also, place a pin in each scallop point (A). Cover the entire item with a towel that is just barely wet (wet the towel in the washer and then spin it dry) (B). Leave the towel in place until the item is completely dry.

3 If desired, blocking wires (long, semiflexible lengths of wire) can be used along straight edges to avoid creating tiny puckers from the pins. The wires are threaded along the straight edges. Instead of pinning the knitting, the wires are held in place using a few pins. This method is quite fast and gives a smoother straight edge.

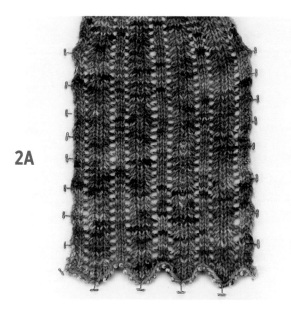

2A

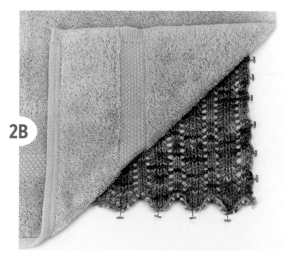

2B

3

STITCH MARKERS

Stitch markers play a very important role in lace knitting. Typically, lace is composed of an identical set of stitches that are repeated over and over across the width of the item. Markers are used to delineate each set of identical stitches. For instance, the Lace Curtain Panels (page 161) are made using a 10-stitch lace pattern that is repeated a total of seven times from side to side. Each 10-stitch section is enclosed by markers. When you reach a marker while knitting a row, slip it from the left needle to the right needle (sm—slip marker) and continue with the next repeat (see page 49 for more information about slipping markers). Until you become proficient with the pattern, at the end of each row, count the stitches to make sure you have the same number between each set of markers. In the case of the curtain panel there should still be 10 stitches between the markers (with a few extra edge stitches). You will quickly memorize which stitch should be coming up in relation to the stitch marker. This will help you to find and correct mistakes within a particular repeat rather than discovering at the end of a row that you have too many or too few stitches.

THREE-NEEDLE BIND-OFF

The three-needle bind-off is used to make a seam and bind off two edges simultaneously. It can be used, for instance, to join two halves of a scarf or join a shoulder seam. **The two pieces being joined must have the same number of stitches.** The third needle that is used for the bind-off step should be one size larger than that used for the knitting. (Note that in the photographs the yarn used for working the stitches is a different color in order to show contrast. You should use the same color yarn as the pieces being joined).

To prepare for the three-needle bind-off, knit the two pieces to be joined through the last row before the bind-off. Because the needle tips must be pointed in the same direction, it will necessitate ending one side on a wrong-side row and the other side on a right-side row. Alternatively, if you are using a circular needle, the stitches of one side can be pushed across the needle so that the needle points and the knit edges line up. This will allow you to end each side on the same row. Don't bind off the stitches but leave them on the needle. The yarn from one of the sides can be cut, leaving a tail at least 8" (20 cm) long. Do not cut the yarn from the other side.

1

1 Place the two pieces of knitting so that the **right sides are together** and the two needles are held parallel to each other with the tips pointing to the right.

2 Insert the third needle into the first stitch on both the front and back needle as if to make a knit stitch.

3 Using the working yarn that remains from the last row of knitting, wrap the yarn around the third needle and draw the loop through both of the stitches on the front and back needles, thus knitting the 2 stitches together and allowing them to slip off the needles.

4 Knit the next 2 stitches (one on the front needle and one on the back needle) in the same manner. There will now be 2 stitches on the third, or right-hand, needle.

5 Using one of the needles in your left hand, pass the right stitch on the third needle over the left stitch (the one closest to the needle tip) and off the end of the needle. One stitch has been bound off.

Repeat steps 2 to 5 until just one loop remains on the third needle. Cut the yarn leaving a tail at least 8" (20 cm) long and pull the cut end through the last stitch to secure it.

How to Knit the Lace Scarf with Beaded Edge

FINISHED DIMENSIONS (FOR EACH SIDE)

- 5½" (14 cm) wide by 61" (155 cm) long

It's easy to modify the width of the scarf. Each repeat of the lace pattern is 7 stitches and about 2" (5 cm) wide. Change the width of the scarf by adding or subtracting stitches in multiples of 7.

KNIT THE SCARF SECTIONS (MAKE TWO ALIKE, EACH USING HALF OF THE TOTAL YARN)

Thread Beads onto the Yarn Using the Big Eye Needle.

1 Before making the cast-on row, 32 beads must be threaded onto the yarn. The big eye beading needle has a large slit (the eye) in the middle. Pry the slit open with your fingernail or another needle and thread the yarn through the needle slit, leaving a short tail.

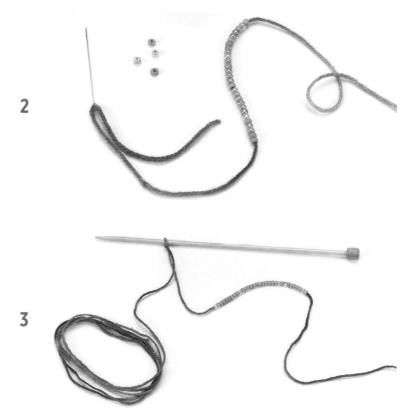

2 Insert the pointed end of the big eye needle through the bead and then slide the bead onto the yarn. Once 32 beads have been strung, remove the beading needle and slide all of the beads at least 1 yd (91 cm) away from the end of the yarn.

3 Make a slip knot in the yarn to the left of the threaded beads and place the slip knot on the knitting needle. The tail for the cast-on (1 yd [91 cm] long)

will be to the left of the slip knot, and the threaded beads and working yarn will be to the right of the slip knot. The beads should be about 8" (20 cm) away from the slip knot.

TIP Slip the stitch markers as you come to them. Until you become comfortable with the pattern, it helps to count the 7 stitches in each section after completion.

Make Beaded Cast-on

Every other cast-on stitch will include a bead. Think of it as working the cast-on stitches in pairs using a two-step process.

Step 1: Cast on 1 st.

Step 2: Slide a bead up against the needle and keep it snug against the needle with the index finger of your right hand (A) while casting on the next stitch with your left hand (B).

   Repeat steps 1 and 2 over and over until all 32 beads have been worked into the cast-on row. End with one more (plain) cast on stitch. You will have 65 stitches (loops) on the needle.

Decrease Stitches and Work Set-up Row

The number of stitches for the scarf must be decreased by half and finally a set-up row is worked to place markers (pm) to delineate the lace pattern repeats.

Row 1: Purl.

Row 2: K1, *k2tog*; repeat from * to * to end of row; 33 sts remain.

Row 3: P1, p2tog, *pm, p7*; repeat from * to * until 2 sts remain, pm, p2; 32 sts remain.

Begin Lace Pattern

The lace pattern itself is an easy 2-row repeat. Each pattern repeat is 7 stitches wide from side to side, and there are 2 stitches at each edge of the scarf.

Row 1 (RS): K1, p1, *sm, k1, yo, ssk, k1, k2tog, yo, k1* repeat from * to * until 2 sts remain, sm, p1, k1.

Row 2: Purl.

   Repeat rows 1 and 2 until half of the yarn is used up (see yarn note above in the What You'll Need). After completing the last row 2, set the first scarf half aside, leaving the stitches on the needle.

   Using the additional set of needles make a second scarf half identical to the first following the steps outlined above for threading the beads onto the yarn, the beaded cast-on, the set-up row, and the lace pattern. For the second scarf section only, one additional row must be completed as follows:

Next row: Knit.

   Leave the stitches of the second scarf half on the needle after completing the additional row.

Join Scarf Halves Together

Hold the scarf halves so that the right sides are together and the two needles are held parallel to each other with the tips pointing to the right. The wrong sides of the knitting distinguished by the bumpy, purl texture will be facing the outside. Using a third needle that is one size larger, work a three-needle bind-off to join the two halves together.

   Block following the directions on page 155 for blocking lace.

Lace Curtain Panels

These scalloped-edged curtain panels are created using a traditional lace pattern known as fishtail lace. The basic pattern can easily be modified to fit any window in your home. The panels are finished with a rod casing at the top.

WHAT YOU'LL LEARN..

- How to make a multiple-row lace pattern with traveling yarnover (yo) holes

- How to make a casing with a turning row and hem

WHAT YOU'LL NEED..

YARN

- Medium weight, smooth yarn, approx. 400 yd (366 m). If possible, find a yarn that has some bamboo or rayon as a portion of the fiber content. This will give the curtain panels better drape.

  Shown: Sirdar Yarns *Snuggly Baby Bamboo* (80% bamboo, 20% wool; 105 yd [96 m] per 1.75 oz [50 g] ball), Willow 133; 4 balls

NEEDLES AND NOTIONS

- US size 7 (4.5 mm) circular needle at least 29" (74 cm) long, or size needed to achieve gauge

- US size 8 (5 mm) straight or circular needle one size larger than smaller needle used to obtain gauge

- Yarn needle for weaving in ends and stitching casing

- Rust-proof pins for blocking

EQUIPMENT

- Iron
- Ironing board
- Curtain rod

GAUGE

- 20 sts = 4" (10 cm) in stockinette stitch

How to Knit the Lace Curtain Panels (make two)

FINISHED DIMENSIONS (FOR EACH SIDE)

- 15" (38 cm) wide by 16" (41 cm) long

It's easy to modify the size of the curtain panels. Each repeat of the lace pattern is 10 stitches and about 2" (5 cm) wide. If you want to make the panel wider, then add stitches in multiples of 10. You can also adjust the length by completing fewer or more repeats of the basic 8-row pattern.

TIP Slip the stitch markers as you come to them. Until you become comfortable with the pattern, it helps to count the 10 stitches in each section after completion.

1 Using the larger needle, **cast on** 75 stitches. Switch to the smaller needle and work a set-up row, placing markers (pm) to delineate the lace pattern repeats, as follows: K2, [pm, k10] 7 times, pm, k3.

2 Begin the fishtail lace pattern. Each repeat is 10 stitches wide from side to side, and 8 rows are required to complete one pattern repeat from bottom to top. When working even-numbered, wrong side (WS) rows, slip markers as you come to them.

Row 1 (RS): K3, *sm, yo, k3, s1, k2tog, psso, k3, yo, k1*; repeat from * to * until 2 sts remain, sm, k2.

Row 2: K3, p until 3 sts remain, k3.

Row 3: K3, *k1, yo, k2, s1, k2tog, psso, k2, yo, k2*; repeat from * to * until 2 sts remain, k2.

Row 4: K3, p until 3 sts remain, k3.

Row 5: K3,*k2, yo, k1, s1, k2tog, psso, k1, yo, k3*; repeat from * to * until 2 sts remain, k2.

Row 6: K3, p until 3 sts remain, k3.

Row 7: K3, *k3, yo, s1, k2tog, psso, yo, k4*; repeat from * to * until 2 sts remain, k2.

Row 8: K3, p until 3 sts remain, k3.

3 You have completed the first full repeat (8 rows) of the lace pattern. Repeat rows 1 through 8 nine more times for a total of ten repeats. Now a short section of stockinette stitch is made to form the front of the casing. All of the markers can be removed at this point. You may find it easier to mark off the first 3 and last 3 stitches with a marker so you can remember to knit them on the wrong-side (purl) rows.

Row 1 (RS): Knit.

Row 2: K3, p until 3 sts remain, k3.

Repeat rows 1 and 2 four more times.

4 A purl row is made on the right side of the knitting. The purl bumps create a turning row, a natural fold line for the knitting.

Next row: Purl.

5 Switch to the larger needles and work a few more rows of stockinette stitch.

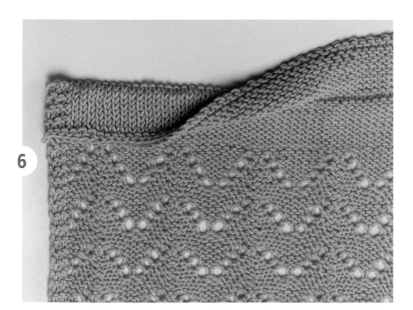

Row 1: K3, p until 3 sts remain, k3.

Row 2: Knit.

Repeat rows 1 and 2 three more times.

Next row: Knit

Bind off all stitches loosely and evenly. Weave in all loose ends.

Curtain Rod Casing

6 To make the casing, fold the top edge along the purl turning row and pin in place.

7 Sew casing into place using a whip stitch: Thread about 1 yd (0.9 m) of yarn on a yarn needle; don't knot the yarn, but leave a tail about 8" (20 cm) that will be woven in later. Starting on the right edge, insert the needle into one bump of a stitch on the wrong side and then into one loop on the cast-off edge. Continue across the edge from right to left working whip stitches between the purl bumps and the cast-off loops. Work a few extra stitches on each edge and then weave in the ends.

Block following the directions on page 155 for blocking lace.

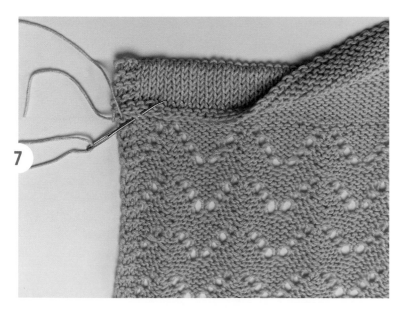

Putting
It Together

By this point you've become a confident knitter who can make scarves, shawls, hats, and more. But what if you want to make something that is the combination of more than one piece? This chapter will teach you how to add a band of knitting to an existing item by picking up stitches. You'll also learn how join two pieces of knitting with a seam.

Directional Blocks Scarf

The unique characteristics of self-striping yarn are used create a scarf with directional blocks. This scarf is made by knitting a narrow center panel and then adding long strips along the sides and finishing with small strips at each narrow end. The technique is somewhat like making a quilt and it can be used with self striping yarns as shown, but it would also be very effective with different colors.

WHAT YOU'LL LEARN. . . . .

- How to achieve different effects from the same self striping yarn

- How to join blocks of knitting by picking up stitches

WHAT YOU'LL NEED. . . . .

YARN

- Medium weight self-striping yarn, approx. 310 yd (283.5 m)

  Shown: Classic Elite Yarns *Liberty Wool* (100% washable wool; 122 yd [111.5 m] per 1.75 oz [50 g] ball); Cloudy Dawn, color 7899, 3 balls

NEEDLES AND NOTIONS

- US size 7 (4.5 mm) 9" (23 cm) single-pointed needles or size needed to achieve gauge

- US size 5 (3.75 mm) circular needle at least 32" (81 cm) long, or two sizes smaller than size needed to achieve gauge

- Yarn needle for weaving in ends

- Rustproof pins for blocking

EQUIPMENT

- Iron

- Ironing board

GAUGE

- 20 sts = 4" (10 cm) in stockinette stitch

The schematic below shows the different sections of the scarf.

End Band	Side Band	End Band
	Center Panel	
	Side Band	

Skills and Useful Information

PICK UP AND KNIT STITCHES

As your knitting progresses, you will often need to add a border or extra section to a piece of knitting that has already been finished. The stitches can be added on the bound-off edge or along the sides, such as a button band on a sweater. Borders and edges are normally worked in stitches that don't curl, such as ribbing, seed stitch, or garter stitch. For the directional block scarf, the technique is used to add the long bands to side of the center panel as well as the two short end bands.

You will most often hear this technique referred to as "pick up and knit stitches," but the words can be confusing. The stitch isn't actually knit as it's being picked up; rather, it is picked up knitwise onto the right needle to be knit (or purled) on the next row. **Stitches are picked up with the right side of the work facing and using a separate ball of yarn.**

1 When picking up stitches along a cast on or bound off edge, insert the right needle from the front to the back, going under two strands along the edge.

2 Wrap the yarn around the needle as if you were knitting and pull a loop through and onto the right needle (2A). You have picked up one stitch. Continue in this manner until the required number of stitches has been added (2B).

The number of stitches to be picked up varies depending on the edge from which you will be working. Typically, if stitches are being picked up from a cast-on or bound-off edge, then 1 stitch should be picked up for each stitch on the edge. After the desired number of stitches have been picked up, then turn the work to the wrong side and continue with the directions (knit, rib, etc.).

3 When picking up stitches along a side edge (or selvedge edge) insert the needle into the space between the first and second stitch. Wrap the yarn around the needle as if you were knitting and pull a loop through onto the right needle.

4 If you are working along a side edge (or selvedge edge) of a scarf or sweater front, then you should not pick up a stitch for every row. Knit stitches are wider than they are tall, so stitches should be picked up in a ratio of about 3 stitches for every 4 rows or 5 stitches for every 7 rows. Don't worry about the space created by skipping a row; it won't be visible after the first row of knit or purl stitches is made. After the desired number of stitches have been picked up, then turn the work to the wrong side and continue with the directions (knit, rib etc.).

WORKING WITH SELF-STRIPING YARN

Self striping yarn is dyed with intervals of changing colors that make stripes when knit. Because the intervals are fixed, for instance, 20 yards of one color connected to 20 yards of the next color, then the height of the stripe remains fairly consistent as long as the width of the knit object remains the same.

The scarf in this pattern has a narrow central panel with tall stripes composed of many rows of the same color. Attached to either side of the center panel are two strips that are knit the long way. Because this section is very wide (thirteen times more stitches than the center panel), it has very short stripes, sometimes 2 rows or less of a color.

When working with self-striping yarn, it is important to remember that the number of stitches in the row will dictate the height of the stripe. If you make a cardigan sweater from self-striping yarn, then you can expect that the back, front, and sleeves will have stripes of differing heights because the width of each of those pieces is different. The scarf also combines stockinette stitch with garter stitch, and you'll notice how different self-striping yarn can look depending on the choice of stitch.

How to Knit the Directional Blocks Scarf

FINISHED DIMENSIONS

- 6" (15 cm) wide by 51" (130 cm) long

1 Knit center panel

Using larger needle, **cast on** 17 sts.

Row 1 (RS): Knit.

Row 2: Purl.

Repeat rows 1 and 2 (stockinette stitch) until length from cast-on edge is approximately 46" (117 cm). Bind off stitches.

2 Pick up stitches for first side block using the smaller needle. Position the center panel with the right side facing you and the length running from side to side. Starting from the right corner and using the smaller needle, pick up and knit 3 stitches for every 4 rows of knitting. Work across the entire long edge; you should have about 225 stitches. Don't worry if your stitch count varies by a few stitches. Your goal should be to pick up somewhere in the neighborhood of 225 stitches.

3 Knit side band. After picking up the stitches for the side band, work 16 rows in garter stitch (knit every row). Bind off from the wrong side. If you have a tendency to bind off tightly (your bound-off edges tend to curve), then use a needle one or two sizes larger for the bind-off needle.

4 Repeat steps 2 and 3 for other side of center panel.

5 Pick up stitches for end bands. Position the scarf with the right side facing you and the short edge up. Starting from the right corner of the short edge of the side band, pick up and knit 8 stitches from the side band, 15 stitches from the center panel, and 8 stitches from the other side band. There should be a total of 31 stitches. When picking up stitches from the side bands, pick up 1 stitch from each garter ridge.

6 Knit end band. After picking up the stitches for the end band, work 16 rows in garter stitch (knit every row). Bind off from the wrong side.

7 Repeat steps 5 and 6 for other end.

8 Finish scarf by weaving in all loose ends and steam blocking following general directions on page 67.

2

5

Baby Bath Robe

Baby items make a terrific first garment. The knitting and finishing are quickly accomplished so the project isn't overwhelming. The other appeal is that the little pieces are always just so cute! This baby bath robe would be the ultimate shower gift—useful yet unusual. It's made from bulky organic cotton that's both soft and absorbent. Instructions begin on page 176.

WHAT YOU'LL LEARN...

- How to choose the correct size pattern
- How to shape a "V" neck
- How to assemble a garment
- How to make seams in knit items
- How to make and attach a belt

WHAT YOU'LL NEED...

YARN

- Bulky weight yarn (preferably cotton or cotton acrylic blend) in two colors in approximate yardage as shown in chart above

  Shown: Classic Elite *Sprout* (100% organic cotton; 109 yd [100 m] per 3.5 oz [100 g] skein)

  Yarn A (as shown on model): Summer Cloud, color 4301, 3 hanks
  Yarn B (as shown on model): Chicory, color 4304, 2 hanks
  Yarn A (as shown in directions): Pea Blossom, color 4354, 3 hanks
  Yarn B (as shown in directions): Summer Cloud, color 4301, 2 hanks

NEEDLES AND NOTIONS

- US size 9 (5.5 mm) 24" (61 cm) circular needle or size needed to achieve gauge for making body pieces*
- US size 7 (4.5 mm) 32" (81 cm) circular needle or two sizes smaller than size used to achieve gauge, for making seed stitch bands
- US size 7 (4.5 mm) 9" (23 cm) single-pointed needles or two sizes smaller than size used to achieve gauge, for making belt

  *The body pieces can be knit on single-pointed needles, but the circular needle is recommended since this yarn is quite heavy and circular needles will be easier on your hands and wrists.

- Yarn needle for weaving in ends
- Locking stitch markers or straight pins
- Two ½" to ¾" (1.5 to 2 cm) buttons
- Sewing needle and thread

EQUIPMENT

- Iron
- Ironing board

GAUGE

- 14 sts = 4" (10 cm) in stockinette stitch

Skills and Useful Information

MAKING SEAMS—MATTRESS STITCH

Many knit garments require a seam of some sort; typically shoulders, sides, and sleeves are seamed. The quality of the seams and finishing on a garment are very important for its overall appeal. It's worth the time to learn how seam neatly and securely. This is a skill that really must be practiced on swatches before sewing the seams on the garment you spent such a long time knitting.

Before seaming, the garment pieces should be blocked to make sure the size and shape match the pattern and also to make the sides smooth and even for easier seaming. In general, the same yarn that was used to knit the pieces should be used to make the seam. Exceptions would be highly textured or very thick yarn, in which case use a thinner yarn of the same fiber type in a matching color. The type of seam taught here is often referred to as the **mattress stitch**. It's a method of

Practice Swatch: Seams

To practice making seams, knit **four** practice swatches using worsted weight yarn and US size 8 (5 mm) 9" (23 cm) single-pointed needles (see pages 6–9 for more information about materials and needles). In the instructions that follow, you will seam the squares with rows running in different orientations, just as you might encounter in an actual garment. The methods vary slightly, so this is a good swatch to keep for reference whenever you need to sew seams.

Cast on 25 sts.

Row 1: Knit.

Row 2: Purl.

Repeat rows 1 and 2 for 26 rows and bind off.

Starting the Seaming Yarn

All three methods use the same technique to start the seaming yarn with a figure 8 between the two sides.

1. Cut a piece of contrasting yarn 24" (61 cm) long and thread it on a yarn needle. Insert the needle from back to front in the lower left corner of the right-hand piece.

2. Leave a tail at least 8" (20 cm) long to be woven in. Form a figure 8 by passing the yarn from back to front in the lower right corner of the left-hand piece.

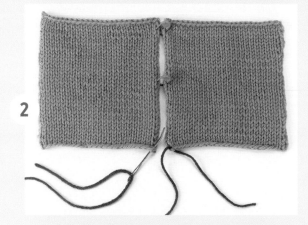

2

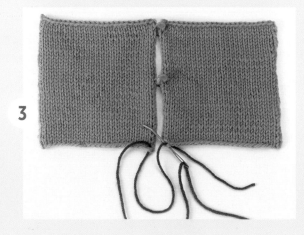

3

3. Next, pass the yarn from back to front through the **same hole** on the right-hand piece where you began.

invisibly seaming by weaving the yarn back and forth between the two sides.

To aid in learning the technique use a contrasting yarn for making the practice seams, but remember that when you sew a garment together you want to use matching yarn. You should work on a flat table with adequate light and a comfortable chair.

USING A ROW COUNTER

The easiest way to make sure the pieces have exactly the same number or rows for seaming

is to use a row counter. Keep track of the number of rows used to make the back using a row counter. When you make the two fronts, be certain they have the same number of rows as the back. You will have an area after the last decrease for the neck shaping to knit even (without increasing or decreasing) where you can adjust the row count to be equal to the back. Likewise, keep track of the number of rows completed to make the first sleeve and make certain the second sleeve matches.

Invisible Seam for Weaving the Vertical (Side) Edges of Stockinette Stitch

This type of seam is used to join side edges.

1. Align the swatches with the right sides facing up and two side edges abutting each other. Use safety pins or locking stitch markers to pin the pieces together and start the seaming yarn as shown above.

2. You are going to be weaving back and forth between the pieces, working one stitch in from the side edge. If you pull the knitting crosswise you will see short horizontal bars between the edge stitch and the second stitch for each row of knitting.

3. Pass the threaded needle under two bars on the left side.

(continued)

4. Next, pass the needle under two bars on the right side.

5. Inserting the needle into the same space from which it exited, continue alternating from side to side. Work upward without skipping any bars. Remove pins as you come to them. When pulling the yarn to tighten, pull in the same direction as the seam and keep the yarn parallel to the flat surface instead of pulling it toward

you. At the end of the seam, pass the threaded needle to the wrong side and make a back stitch or two in the seam. Finish by weaving in the ends securely.

TIP If the two pieces you are seaming are not exactly symmetrical, you can compensate by passing the threaded needle under two bars on the longer piece and one bar on the shorter piece until the extra length is eased.

Invisible Seam for Weaving the Horizontal (Bound-off) Edges of Stockinette Stitch

This type of seam is used to join shoulder seams.

1. Align the swatches with right sides facing up and the bound-off edges abutting each other with the stitches lined up.

2. Use safety pins or locking stitch markers to pin the pieces together, and start the seaming yarn as shown on page 172. Pass the threaded needle under the two legs of the "V" formed by a stitch inside of the bound-off edge.

(continued)

3. Pass the threaded needle under the corresponding stitch inside of the bound-off edge on the opposite side. Pull the yarn tightly enough to make the bound-off edge roll to the inside and form a seam.

Continue working from side to side until the seam has been joined. At the end of the seam, pass the threaded needle to the wrong side and make a back stitch or two in the seam. Finish by weaving in the ends securely.

Invisible Seam for Weaving a Vertical (Side) Edge to a Horizontal (Bound-off) Edge of Stockinette Stitch

This type of seam is used to join stitches to rows such as joining the top of a sleeve to an armhole or shoulder edge.

1. Align the swatches with right sides facing up and the bound-off edge of one swatch abutting the side edge of the other.

2. Use safety pins or locking stitch markers to pin the pieces together and start the seaming yarn as shown on page 172. Pass the threaded needle under one or two bars on the side edge.*

3. Pass the threaded needle under the two legs of the "V" formed by a stitch inside of the bound-off edge.

4. Continue working side to side from rows to stitches. At the end of the seam, pass the threaded needle to the wrong side and make a back stitch or two in the seam. Finish by weaving in the ends securely.

*Since there are more rows than stitches, it will be necessary to compensate by occasionally passing the threaded needle under two bars on the side edge instead of one.

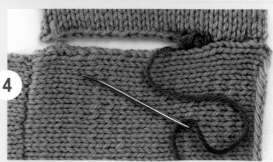

How to Make the Baby Bath Robe

Sizes and Finished Dimensions

	Size 1	Size 2	Size 3
To Fit Size	12 month	18 month	24 month
To Fit Chest Size	20" (51 cm)	21" (53 cm)	22" (56 cm)
Actual Garment Chest Measurement	24" (61 cm)	25" (63.5 cm)	26" (66 cm)
Length	17" (43 cm)	19" (48 cm)	21" (53 cm)
Yardage Required Yarn A	275 yd (251 m)	320 yd (292 m)	365 yd (334 m)
Yardage Required Yarn B	110 yd (101 m)	130 yd (119 m)	145 yd (133 m)

- Directions are shown as Size 1 (Size 2, Size 3). Note that the size numbers (1, 2, and 3) are not the same as children's clothing sizes. This numbering system is used to make the patterns easier to read.

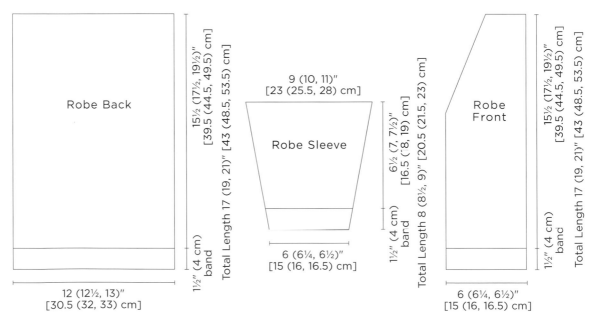

Above is a schematic of the individual pieces showing the finished dimensions of each piece. The measurements use the same organization as the directions: Size 1 (Size 2, Size 3)

PATTERN SIZING

Clothing items are usually made with some ease, which is the difference between the actual measurements of the garment compared to the measurement of the body it is designed to fit. The baby bathrobe has an ease of 4" (10 cm); the actual garment chest measurement of the 12 month size is 24" (61 cm) even though the average chest measurement of a 12-month-old baby is 20" (51 cm).

This pattern is written for a range of sizes, so it will be necessary to determine which directions apply to the size you are making. The chart on page 176 defines the dimensions of a particular size. The chart not only suggests the size (12 months, for instance) but also states the average chest size of a 12-month-old baby (20" [51 cm]). Please

take note that the size numbers (1, 2, and 3) used in the chart and pattern are not the same as children's clothing sizes. This numbering system is used to make the patterns easier to read.

Back

1 Using larger needle and yarn A **cast on** 42 (44, 46) sts. Purl the next row. See note on page 173 about using a row counter.

2 Work remainder of body in stockinette stitch as follows:

Row 1: Knit.

Row 2: Purl.

Repeat rows 1 and 2 until the length from the cast-on row is 15½" (17½", 19½ ") [39.5 cm (44.5 cm, 49.5 cm)]. Bind off and cut the yarn, leaving a tail at least 8" (20 cm) long.

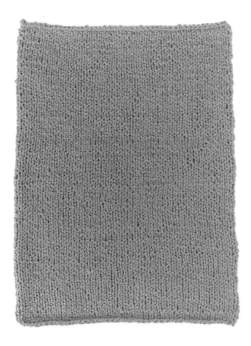

2

Right Front

(You are making the right front as worn on the body.)

3 Using larger needle and yarn A **cast on** 21 (22, 23) sts. Purl the next row.

4 Work body in stockinette stitch as follows:

Row 1: Knit.

Row 2: Purl.

Repeat rows 1 and 2 until the length from the cast-on row is 11" (12½", 14") [28 cm (32 cm, 35.5 cm)]. Before beginning the neckline decreases below, be certain that you have just finished a purl row.

5 Decrease along neck edge. **Note:** rows 11 and 12 are skipped for size 1 because of its fewer number of stitches.

Row 1: K1, ssk, knit to end of row—20 (21, 22) sts remain.

Row 2: Purl.

Row 3: K1, ssk, knit to end of row—19 (20, 21) sts remain.

Row 4: Purl.

Row 5: K1, ssk, knit to end of row—18 (19, 20) sts remain.

Row 6: Purl.

Row 7: K1, ssk, knit to end of row—17 (18, 19) sts remain.

(continued)

Row 8: Purl.

Row 9: K1, ssk, knit to end of row—16 (17, 18) sts remain.

Row 10: Purl.

Row 11 for sizes 2 and 3 only (Skip this row for size 1): K1, ssk, knit to end of row—(16, 17) sts remain.

Row 12 for sizes 2 and 3 only (Skip this row for size 1): Purl.

Row 13: Knit.

Row 14: Purl.

Row 15: K1, ssk, knit to end of row—15 (15, 16) sts remain.

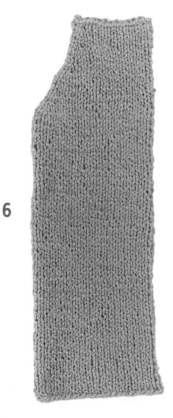

6

Row 16: Purl.

Row 17: Knit.

Row 18: Purl.

6 Repeat rows 17 and 18 until the length from the cast-on edge is 15½" (17½", 19½") [39.5 cm (44.5 cm, 49.5 cm)). Bind off and cut the yarn, leaving a tail at least 8" (20 cm) long.

Left Front
(You are making the left front as worn on the body.)

7 Using larger needle and yarn A **cast on** 21 (22, 23) sts. Purl the next row.

8 Work body as follows:

Row 1: Knit.

Row 2: Purl.

Repeat rows 1 and 2 until the length from the cast-on row is 11" (12½", 14") [28 cm (32 cm, 35.5 cm)]. Before beginning the neckline decreases below, be certain that you have just finished a purl row.

9 Decrease along neck edge. **Note:** rows 11 and 12 are skipped for size 1 because of its fewer number of stitches.

Row 1: Knit until 3 sts remain, k2tog, k1—20 (21, 22) sts remain.

Row 2: Purl.

Row 3: Knit until 3 sts remain, k2tog, k1—19 (20, 21) sts remain.

Row 4: Purl.

Row 5: Knit until 3 sts remain, k2tog, k1—18 (19, 20) sts remain.

Row 6: Purl.

Row 7: Knit until 3 sts remain, k2tog, k1—17 (18, 19) sts remain.

Row 8: Purl.

Row 9: Knit until 3 sts remain, k2tog, k1—16 (17, 18) sts remain.

Row 10: Purl.

Row 11 for sizes 2 and 3 only (Skip this row for size 1): Knit until 3 sts remain, k2tog, k1—(16, 17) sts remain.

Row 12 for sizes 2 and 3 only (Skip this row for size 1): Purl.

Row 13: Knit.

Row 14: Purl.

Row 15: Knit until 3 sts remain, k2tog, k1—15 (15, 16) sts remain.

Row 16: Purl.

Row 17: Knit.

Row 18: Purl.

10 Repeat rows 17 and 18 until the length from the cast-on edge is 15½" (17½", 19½") [39.5 cm (44.5 cm, 49.5 cm)]. Bind off and cut the yarn leaving a tail at least 8" (20 cm) long.

Sleeves (make two)

11 Cuff: using smaller needle and yarn B, **cast on** 23 (23, 25) sts. When making cast-on row, leave a tail at least 10" (25.5 cm) long that will later be used to seam the cuff. Work cuff in seed stitch as follows:

Row 1: *K1, p1*; repeat from * to * until 1 st remains, k1.

Repeat row 1 eight more times for a total of 9 rows.

12 Sleeve shaping: shape sleeves by working increases along each edge. From this point, each sleeve has a unique set of directions. Follow the directions for the size you are making.

Size 1

Change to larger needles and yarn A.

12

Row 1: K11, k2tog, k10—22 sts remain.

Row 2: Purl.

Row 3: Knit.

Row 4: Purl.

Row 5: K1, M1R, knit until 1 st remains, M1L, k1—24 sts.

Row 6: Purl.

Row 7: Knit.

Row 8: Purl.

Row 9: K1, M1R, knit until 1 st remains, M1L, k1—26 sts.

Row 10: Purl.

Row 11: Knit.

Row 12: Purl.

Row 13: Knit.

Row 14: Purl.

Row 15: K1, M1R, knit until 1 st remains, M1L, k1—28 sts.

Rows 16 to 21: Repeat rows 11 to 15—30 sts after completing row 21.

Rows 22 to 27: Repeat rows 11 to 15—32 sts after completing row 27.

After completing row 32, the length from the cast-on row should be 8" (20 cm). If necessary, add or subtract rows after the last increase (row 27) in order to reach the correct length.

Row 28: Purl.

Row 29: Knit.

Row 30: Purl.

Row 31: Knit.

Row 32: Purl.

Bind off and cut the yarn, leaving a tail at least 8" (20 cm) long.

Size 2

Change to larger needles and yarn A.

Row 1: K11, k2tog, k10—22 sts remain.

Row 2: Purl.

Row 3: Knit.

(continued)

Row 4: Purl.

Row 5: K1, M1R, knit until 1 st remains, M1L, k1—24 sts.

Row 6: Purl.

Row 7: Knit.

Row 8: Purl.

Row 9: K1, M1R, knit until 1 st remains, M1L, k1—26 sts.

Rows 10 to 13: Repeat rows 6 to 9—28 sts after completing row 13.

Rows 14 to 17: Repeat rows 6 to 9—30 sts after completing row 17.

Rows 18 to 21: Repeat rows 6 to 9—32 sts after completing row 21.

Rows 22 to 25: Repeat rows 6 to 9—34 sts after completing row 25.

Row 26: Purl.

Row 27: Knit.

Row 28: Purl.

Row 29: Knit.

Row 30: Purl.

Row 31: K1, M1R, knit until 1 st remains, M1L, k1—36 sts.

After completing row 36, length from the cast-on row should be 8½" (21.5 cm). If necessary, add or subtract rows after the last increase (row 31) in order to reach the correct length.

Row 32: Purl.

Row 33: Knit.

Row 34: Purl.

Row 35: Knit.

Row 36: Purl.

Bind off and cut the yarn, leaving a tail at least 8" (20 cm) long.

Size 3

Change to larger needles and yarn A.

Row 1: K11, k2tog, k10—24 sts remain.

Row 2: Purl.

Row 3: Knit.

Row 4: Purl.

Row 5: K1, M1R, knit until 1 st remains, M1L, k1—26 sts.

Row 6: Purl.

Row 7: Knit.

Row 8: Purl.

Row 9: K1, M1R, knit until 1 st remains, M1L, k1—28 sts.

Rows 10 to 13: Repeat rows 6 to 9—30 sts after completing row 13.

Rows 14 to 17: Repeat rows 6 to 9—32 sts after completing row 17.

Rows 18 to 21: Repeat rows 6 to 9—34 sts after completing row 21.

Row 22: Purl.

Row 23: Knit.

Row 24: Purl.

Row 25: Knit.

Row 26: Purl.

Row 27: K1, M1R, knit until 1 st remains, M1L, k1—36 sts.

Rows 28 to 33: Repeat rows 22 to 27—38 sts after completing row 21.

After completing row 38, the length from the cast-on row should be 9" (23 cm). If necessary, add or subtract rows after the last increase (row 33) in order to reach the correct length.

Row 34: Purl.

Row 35: Knit.

Row 36: Purl.

Row 37: Knit.

Row 38: Purl.

Bind off and cut the yarn, leaving a tail at least 8" (20 cm) long.

Lightly steam all pieces following directions on page 67. The pieces should be as smooth and flat as possible and the measurements should conform to those shown in the schematics on page 176.

HOW TO ASSEMBLE THE ROBE

13 The robe pieces will be joined in stages. After each seam is completed, steam it lightly to ensure that it lies as flat as possible before the next piece is joined.

14 Begin by joining the fronts to the back at the shoulder seam. Align the left front so that the bound-off edge adjoins the bound-off edge of the shoulder and pin to secure with locking stitch markers or straight pins. The selvedge edges should be lined up on the right side and the neck shaping should face to the left.

15 Cut a length of yarn A about 18" (45.5 cm) long and thread onto a yarn needle. Sew the shoulder seam together using the mattress stitch for bound-off edges (page 175). Leave a tail at least 8" (20 cm) long at the beginning and remove pins as you work. When the seam is finished weave, in the ends to secure.

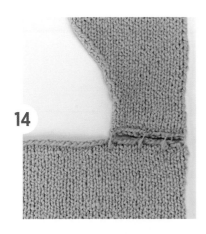

14

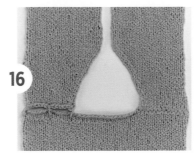

16

16 Align the right front to mirror the left front and join the shoulder seam.

17 Mark the center point of the bound-off top edge of the sleeve.

18 Align the center with the shoulder seam. Pin the sleeve to the front and back sides. The distance from the sleeve center point to the sleeve side edge should be 4½" (5", 5⅜") [11.5 cm (12.5 cm, 13.5 cm).

19 Cut a length of yarn A about 18" (45.5 cm) long and thread on to a yarn needle. Join the sleeve to the body using the mattress stitch for bound-off edges to side edges (page 175). Leave a tail at least 8" (20 cm) long at the beginning and remove pins as you work.

18

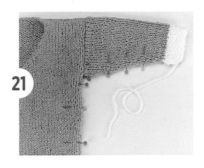

21

When the seam is finished, weave in the ends to secure.

20 Repeat for other sleeve.

21 Working one side at a time, pin the front to the back to make a seam and pin the sleeve edges to make a seam. The underarm and side will be sewn as one continuous seam.

22 Cut a length of yarn A about 30" (76 cm) long and thread on to a yarn needle. Sew the seam using the mattress stitch for side edges (page 174). Begin sewing on the sleeve seam above the cuff. Leave a tail at least 8" (20 cm) long at the beginning and remove pins as you work. When the seam is finished, weave in the ends to secure.

23 Using the long tail from the cast-on of the cuff, join the short cuff seam. Work from side to side in a modified mattress stitch: catching the purl bumps that are on the selvedge edge, which gives a flatter seam that won't be seen when the

(continued)

23

cuffs are turned up. When the seam is finished, weave in the ends to secure.

CONTRAST BORDER

24 To make bottom contrast border, pick up stitches from the cast-on edge beginning with the center edge of the left front. As a basic guide, pick up approximately 1 stitch for each cast-on stitch on the edge. It isn't necessary to pick up exactly the same number as shown in the guide below. Just be certain you have an odd number of stitches after all the stitches have been picked up. If not, simply adjust the spacing between the last few stitches (either one stitch closer or further away). Pick up stitches as follows:

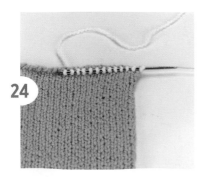

24

Size 1: Total of 81 sts: 20 from left front, 41 from back, 20 from right front.

Size 2: Total of 85 sts: 21 from left front, 43 from back, 21 from right front.

Size 3: Total of 89 sts: 22 from left front, 45 from back, 22 from right front.

25 Work band in seed stitch as follows:

Row 1: *K1, p1*; repeat from * to * until 1 st remains, k1.

Repeat row 1 seven more times for a total of 8 rows. Bind off in pattern. Cut yarn, leaving a tail at least 8" (20 cm) long.

26 Stitches are picked up for the continuous band that is attached to the center front and neck edges. It isn't necessary to pick up exactly the same number as shown in the guide below. Just be certain you have an odd number of stitches after all the stitches have been picked up. If not, simply adjust the spacing between the last few stitches (either 1 row closer or further away).

When making the center front and neck edge border, pick up stitches from the side (selvedge edge) beginning with the bottom corner of the right center front (A). As a general guide, pick up about 5 stitches for every 8 rows along the center front.

The best way to determine the spacing of the picked up stitches along the angled portion of the neck shaping is to divide the distance in half (or even quarters) and mark with pins. When picking up stitches along this edge, divide the number to be picked up among the sections marked with the pins. The neck edge includes the space taken up by the shoulder seams (B). Along the back of the neck, pick up approximately 1 stitch for each bound-off stitch (C). Pick up stitches as follows:

A

B

C

Size 1: Total of 141 sts: 45 from right center front, 19 from right angled neck line, 14 from center back, 19 from left angled neck line, and 44 from left center front.

Size 2: Total of 157 sts: 49 from right center front, 22 from right angled neck line, 16 from center back, 22 from left angled neck line, and 48 from left center front.

Size 3: Total of 171 sts: 54 from right center front, 24 from right angled neck line, 16 from center back, 24 from left angled neck line, and 53 from left center front.

27 Work band in seed stitch as follows:

Row 1: *K1, p1*; repeat from * to * until 1 st remains, k1.

Repeat row 1 seven more times for a total of 8 rows. Bind off in pattern. Cut yarn leaving a tail at least 8" (20 cm) long.

28 Make the belt. Using the smaller single-pointed needles and yarn B, cast on 6 sts. Work the belt in rib stitch as follows:

Row 1: *K1, p1*; repeat from * to * to end of row.

Repeat row 1 until the belt is 36" (37", 38") [91.5 cm (94 cm, 96.5 cm]) long. Bind off in pattern and cut yarn, leaving a tail at least 8" (20 cm) long. Weave in all ends.

29 Lay the robe out so the back is flat and smooth.

With a straight pin, mark a distance on each side seam that is 7" (7½", 8") [18 cm (19 cm, 20 cm]) down from the shoulder seam. Measuring between these two marks, find the center back and mark it with a straight pin.

30 Position the center of the belt on the center back and be certain that the belt is parallel to the bottom and centered widthwise over the marks on the side seam. Pin the center and then pin 3" (7.5 cm) to each side of center.

31 Thread about 18" (45.5 cm) of yarn A on yarn needle. Knot the yarn and use a running stitch to attach the belt securely at each position which is marked 3" (7.5 cm) to the side of the center back.

32 Use sewing thread and needle to attach buttons.

33 Gently steam all bands and seams a final time. Sew in all loose ends.

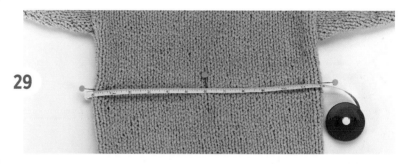

29

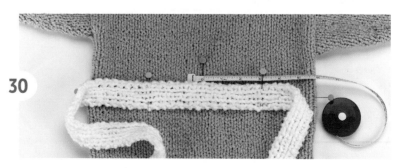

30

31

Baby Hat with Button Band

Why not use the leftover yarn from the baby bath robe to make an adorable hat? Or make the hat by itself; you couldn't find a softer or cuter gift for a little person.

WHAT YOU'LL LEARN . . . .

- How to make a baby hat with a contrast button band

WHAT YOU'LL NEED . . . .

YARN

- Bulky weight yarn (preferably cotton or cotton acrylic blend) in two colors in approximate yardage as shown in chart on page 186

Shown: The hat uses the same yarn as the Baby Bath Robe: Classic Elite *Sprout* (100% organic cotton; 109 yd [100 m] per 3.5 oz [100 g] skein). If you are also making the robe you should have enough of yarn A remaining to make the hat. You will most likely need to purchase an additional hank of yarn B for the hat, but don't wind that hank into a ball until you are certain you need it. Your LYS or craft store won't allow you to return yarn that has been wound into a ball.

Yarn A (as shown on model): Summer Cloud, color 4301, 1 hank
Yarn B (as shown on model): Chicory, color 4304, 1 hank
Yarn A (as shown in directions): Pea Blossom, color 4354, 1 hank
Yarn B (as shown in directions): Summer Cloud, color 4301, 1 hank

NEEDLES AND NOTIONS

- US size 9 (5.5 mm) 16" (41 cm) circular needle or size needed to achieve gauge

- US size 7 (4.5 mm) single-pointed needles or two sizes smaller than size used to achieve gauge

- US size 9 (5.5 mm) 7" (18 cm) double-pointed needles or same size used to achieve gauge

  If you prefer, the smaller size can be worked on a 12" (30.5 cm) circular needle or entirely on double-pointed needles

- Yarn needle for weaving in ends

- One ½" to ¾" (1.3 to 2 cm) button

- Sewing needle and thread

GAUGE

- 14 sts = 4" (10 cm) in stockinette stitch

How to Knit the Baby Hat

Size and Finished Dimensions

	Size 1	Size 2	Size 3
To Fit Size	12 month	18 month	24 month
Hat Circumference	13¾" (35 cm)	16" (40.5 cm)	17¼" (44 cm)
Hat Height	6" (15 cm)	7" (18 cm)	8" (20.5 cm)
Yardage Required Yarn A	17 yd (15 m)	20 yd (18 m)	21 yd (19 m)
Yardage Required Yarn B	39 yd (36 m)	45 yd (41.5 m)	49 yd (45 m)

- Directions are shown as Size 1 (Size 2, Size 3). Note that the size numbers (1, 2, and 3) are not the same as children's clothing sizes. This numbering system is used to make the patterns easier to read.

1 The button band is knit as a flat piece working back and forth in rows instead of joining in the round.

Using yarn B and the smaller needle, **cast on** 53 (61, 65) sts.

Row 1: K1, *p1, k1* until 1 st remains, k1.

Repeat row 1 seven more times for a total of 8 rows.

2 Bind off 5 sts. Cut yarn A and change to yarn B, leaving tails at least 8" (20 cm) long. Transfer single stitch (left from the bind off) on right needle to the circular needle and then continue across the row, working all stitches in knit stitch. As you work across the row, the stitches will be knit off the single-point needle onto the circular needle—48 (56, 60) sts remain on needle.

2

3

3 Bring the tips of the circular needle together, keeping the bound-off button tab free. The stitch with the working yarn attached should be on the right. Slip a BOR marker on the right needle. Insert the right needle into the first stitch on the left needle and make a stitch using the working yarn, thereby joining the hat in the round.

4 Continue working stockinette stitch in the round (knit every stitch), slipping the BOR marker as you work until the height from the cast-on row is 4½" (5", 5½") [11.5 cm (12.5 cm, 14 cm)].

5 Begin decreases to shape the crown of the hat. The larger the size, the more stitches in the hat. So, the larger sizes will require more rounds to decrease their greater number of stitches. If you are making one of the smaller sizes, then skip the rounds that don't apply to your hat. Change to double-pointed needles when the stitches will no longer fit comfortably around the circular needle.

Round 1 for size 3 only: *K13, k2tog*; repeat from * to * to end of round—56 sts remain. Skip this round for other sizes.

Round 2 for size 3 only: Knit. Skip this round for other sizes.

Round 3 for sizes 2 and 3 only: *K5, k2tog*; repeat from * to * to end of round—48 sts remain. Skip this round for size 1.

Round 4 for sizes 2 and 3 only: Knit. Skip this round for size 1.

From this point on all sizes are worked the same.

Round 5: *K4, k2tog*; repeat from * to * to end of round—40 sts remain.

Round 6: Knit.

Round 7: *K3, k2tog*; repeat from * to * to end of round—32 sts remain.

Round 8: Knit.

Round 9: *K2, k2tog*; repeat from * to * to end of round—24 sts remain.

Round 10: Knit.

Round 11: *K1, k2tog*; repeat from * to * to end of round—16 sts remain.

Round 12: Knit.

Round 13: *K2tog*; repeat from * to * to end of round—8 sts remain.

6 Cut the yarn leaving a tail at least 8" (20 cm) long. Using a yarn needle, thread the tail through the remaining stitches and pass it through the hole in the top of the hat to the inside. Pull the tail firmly to close the hole and weave the ends into the stitches on the inside to secure. Weave in all other ends.

7 To finish the hat band, overlap the button tab and pin into place. Use sewing needle and thread to attach the button and secure the button tab in place. Lightly steam following directions on page 67.

6

Troubleshooting

You will inevitably make a mistake here and there in your knitting. A stitch might get dropped or twisted, but the important thing is to not panic. Unless you are knitting with slippery silk, the slightly fuzzy surface of the yarn strand will most likely keep the stitch from running to the bottom of your knitting and creating a disaster.

TWISTED STITCH

An important characteristic to recognize is the proper orientation of a stitch. A knit stitch, or loop, forms an upside-down "U" shape. As the "U" is sitting on the needle the right leg, or leading leg, should be on the front side of the needle and the left leg should be behind the needle. Think of the stitch as a gymnast sitting on a balance beam: her right leg is in front of the beam while her left leg is behind the beam.

When a stitch is twisted (as shown at right), the left leg of the "U" falls in front of the needle with the right leg behind. You'll often feel a twisted stitch before you see it clearly because it just doesn't feel right when you insert your needle into the loop to make a new stitch.

Twisted stitch

1 To correct a twisted stitch, insert the right needle into the stitch from behind the loop.

2 Pull the loop off the left needle.

3 Put the loop back on to the left needle with the correct orientation.

WHY IS MY STITCH COUNT INCREASING?

This is a very common complaint from new knitters. As they work on a knit item, the number of stitches on their needle gradually increases, and before they know it they've made a wedge instead of a neat rectangle.

Incorrect

Correct

Incorrect! The reason this happens is because of the way the working yarn on the first stitch of the row is treated. When a knitter finishes the last stitch and turns the needle to begin a new row they take the working yarn over the top of the needle and pull it down to the back to begin the new row. This pulls the bump at the bottom of the stitch over the top of the needle and gives it the appearance of two strands or loops to be knit.

Correct! At the end of every row, the working yarn should exit the bump at the bottom of the stitch in front of the needle. Get into the habit of gently pulling all of your stitches down away from the needle at the end of every row (and giving them a once-over to make sure there are no problems).

DROPPED STITCH

When a stitch loop falls off the needle, it will gradually drop down row by row. As it drops, each loop that falls out will make a horizontal strand behind the loop. This is exactly the same as what happens when a run occurs in a pair of tights. This is normally a very gradual process and you will usually have plenty of time to correct the problem, so don't panic!

The best tool for fixing a dropped stitch is a crochet hook that is small enough to fit easily through the loop of the stitch.

(continued)

1 Working from the front to the back, insert the hook through the loop and under the horizontal strand.

2 Using the hook, catch the horizontal strand behind the dropped stitch and pull it through the loop of the dropped stitch.

3 Again using the hook, place the loop on the needle in the proper orientation, making sure the right leg of the stitch falls in front of the needle.

UN-KNITTING OR TAKING OUT STITCHES

The sign of a good knitter is his or her acceptance and confidence when it becomes necessary to take out an incorrect stitch or even several rows of stitches to get back to a section which must be corrected. This is often referred to as un-knitting or ripping out. The most colorful term is frogging (rip-it, rip-it).

The process of un-knitting is reversing the actions that happened to the stitches on the right needle.

1 To un-knit a stitch, insert the left needle into the front of the stitch in the row below the stitch or loop on the right needle. Another way to think of this is inserting the left needle into the hole from which the loop on the right needle is exiting.

2 Keeping the left needle in the stitch below, pull the right needle out of the stitch on the needle.

3 Gently pull the working yarn out of the stitch. Repeat for as many stitches as necessary.

If it becomes necessary to un-knit several rows of knitting, then take the entire work off the needle and pull the working yarn to unravel the knitting row by row until you've reached the point that is 1 row above the row that requires correction. Return the live stitches to a needle and un-knit the final row stitch by stitch following the directions above.

TIP Check out the accompanying DVD for more troubleshooting techniques and tips.

About the Author

Carri Hammett is a prolific designer and writer who got her start by designing for customers in the yarn shop she opened in 2002. She loves to collaborate with both readers and customers as together they express their love of knitting and expand their knitting knowledge and skill. Carri sold her shop in 2010 so she could focus her energy on writing and expanding her online sales. She is also the author of Scarves and Shawls for Yarn Lovers, Mittens and Hats for Yarn Lovers, and Ready, Set, Knit Cables.

Carri lives in Minnesota with her husband; her three kids all live too far away but at least they all learned how to knit before they moved out. She loves to hear from readers! You can send Carri an email at carri@coldwateryarn.com

Abbreviations

Here is the list of standard abbreviations used for knitting. Until you can readily identify them, keep the list handy whenever you knit.

6-st LKC	six-stitch left knit cross (p. 63)	psso	pass slipped stitch over (p. 154)
6-st RKC	six-stitch right knit cross (p. 64)	Rev St st	reverse stockinette stitch (p. 45)
BO	bind off (p. 20)	rm	remove marker (p. 49)
BOR	beginning of round (p. 103)	RS	right side
cm	centimeter	WS	wrong side
CO	cast on (p. 16)	sl	slip
dpn(s)	double pointed needles	sm	slip marker (p. 49)
g	gram	ssk	slip, slip, knit (p. 81)
K, k	knit (p. 18)	st	stitch
k2tog	knit two together (p. 66, 80)	sts	stitches
kf&b	knit front and back (p. 65, 75)	St st	stockinette stitch (p. 45)
LYS	local yarn shop	wyib	with yarn in back (p. 132)
m	meter	wyif	with yarn in front (p. 132)
mm	millimeter	yd	yard(s)
M1L	make one left (p. 78)	yo	yarnover (p. 78)
M1R	make one right (p. 77)	* *	repeat instructions between * as directed (p. 54)
P, p	purl (p. 44)		
p2tog	purl two together (p. 81)	[ ]	repeat instructions enclosed by brackets as directed (p. 50)
pf&b	purl front and back (p. 76)		
pm	place marker (p. 49)	"	inch(es)

Index

A
assembling pieces, 181–182

B
Baby Bath Robe, 171–183
Baby Blocks Blanket, 43–51
Baby Hat with Button Band, 185–187
bias knitting, 139
binding off, 14, 20, 58–59, 133, 156–157
blocking, 50, 67, 133, 154–155
bobbles, 85
borders, 168, 182–183

C
cable cast-on, 47, 82
Cabled Smart Phone Case, 61–69
cables, 41, 61, 62–65
casting on, 14, 16–17, 47, 48, 82
circular needles, 48, 99, 102–104
color, 125–149
Color Blend Scarf, 137–141
Color Block Hat, 143–149
color charts, 145
Continental method, 54, 56
crochet chain, 83

D
damp blocking, 50
decreases, 65–67, 74, 80–82, 93, 154
Directional Block Scarf, 167–169
double-point needles, 9, 112–113, 118–119
dropped stitch, 189–190
duplicate stitch, 146, 149

E
Easy Knit Hat, 111–115
ends, weaving in, 22–23
English method, 54, 55

F
Felted Bag with Embellished Flap, 101–109
Felted Christmas Tree, 73–91
felting, 73, 82–83, 104–105, 107–109
fishtail lace, 161–163
fringe, 36–37, 39

G
garter stitch, 24
Garter Stitch Scarf, 13–27
gauge swatch, 25
Golf Club Covers, 117–123

H
hats, 143–149, 185–187

I
I-cord, 84
increases, 65–67, 74–79, 93

K
knit front and back (kf&b), 65–66, 75
knit stitch, 18–19, 45, 46
knitting, 14

knitting in the round, 102–123
knitting needles, 8–9
   circular, 48, 99, 102–104
   double-point, 9, 112–113, 118–119
   methods of holding, 54–56
knit two together (k2tog), 66–67, 80

L
lace, 151–163
Lace Curtain Panels, 161–163
Lace Scarf with Beaded Edge, 153–159
Leaf Edge Shawl, 93–97
left knit cross (LKC), 62, 63
long-tail cast-on, 14
Loosely Knit Scarf, 29–31

M
make one (M1), 77
make one left (M1L), 78
make one right (M1R), 77
mattress stitch, 172–173

N
needle felting, 104–105, 107–109
needle sizes, 9, 25, 30–31

P
pass slipped stitch over (PSSO), 154
patterns
   binding off in, 58–59
   modifying, 50, 59, 67
   in multiples of stitches, 134
   reading, 50, 54, 146
   sizing, 177
   slip stitch, 132, 134
pick up and knit stitches, 168
picot bind-off, 133
place marker, 49
pompoms, 120–121
practice swatches, 4, 18–19, 44–46, 55–58, 65, 79, 82, 102–103, 118–119, 144, 172–175
purl front and back (pf&b), 76
purl stitch, 41, 44, 46, 55, 56
purl two together (p2tog), 81

R
remove marker, 49
ribbing, 58
right knit cross (RKC), 62, 64
row, 14
row counter, 173

S
Scarf Knit with Two Yarns, 33–39
scarves, 13–27, 29–31, 33–39, 137–141, 153–159
seams, 172–175
seed stitch, 53, 57
Seed Stitch Table Runner, 53–59
self-striping yarn, 168–169
shaping, 71
shawls, 93–97, 131–135
single-point needles, 8–9

six-stitch left knit cross (6-st LKC), 63
six-stitch right knit cross (6-st RKC), 64
slip, slip knit (ssk), 81
slip knot, 14–15
slip marker, 49
slip stitch, 131, 132, 134
Slip Stitch Shawl, 131–135
steam blocking, 58, 67
stitch count, 189
stitches
   dropped, 189–190
   duplicate stitch, 146, 149
   garter stitch, 24
   height and width differences, 50
   increases and decreases, 65–67, 74–82, 93, 154
   knit stitch, 18–19, 45, 46
   mattress stitch, 172–173
   picking up, 168
   purl stitch, 41, 44, 46, 55, 56
   seed stitch, 53, 57
   slip stitch, 131, 132, 134
   stockinette stitch, 45, 104
   switching between, 46
   taking out, 190
   twisted, 188
stitch markers, 49, 156
stockinette stitch, 45, 104
stranded knitting, 144
Striped Cotton Bathroom Rug, 127–129
stripes, 128

T
tails, 14, 22–23
texture, 6, 41, 46, 62
three-needle bind-off, 156–157
tools, 8–9
troubleshooting, 188–190
twisted stitch, 188

U
un-knitting, 190

W
weaving in ends, 22–23
wet blocking, 133
working yarn, 14

Y
yarn, 6–8
   classification of, 34
   combining, 34–35
   joining new, 21
   knitting with two, 36
   labels, 7–8, 30
   methods of holding, 54, 55–56
   packaging, 7
   self-striping, 168–169
   texture, 6
   weight, 6–7, 34
yarnover (yo), 78